CAREEREALISM

THE SMART APPROACH TO A SATISFYING CAREER

By J.T. O'Donnell

First published by Dog Ear Publishing
4010 W. 86th Street, Ste H
Indianapolis, IN 46268
www.dogearpublishing.net

ISBN: 978-159858-601-5

This book is printed on acid-free paper.

Printed in the United States of America

Author's Note

If you are considering reading this book, then you've most likely been contemplating your career quite a bit lately. Maybe you are a working individual who is thinking twice about your current job's ability to satisfy your needs. Or, perhaps you are just starting out in your career and are overwhelmed by the complexity of finding a job that will make you feel successful. Whatever the reason, one thing is certain: Work, as you define it, is not working for you!

I'm here to tell you that your dissatisfaction is not isolated. A recent survey by *Yahoo HotJobs* indicates 7 out of 10 Americans are unhappy at work. So how is it that a society like ours, highly educated and with one of the best standards-of-living in the world, struggles to feel professionally satisfied? The answer lies in a history lesson.

Let's start by stating an important fact: Career success is the American Way. We are a country that was founded on 'rags-to-riches' stories that have paved the path for people of all backgrounds to come and make their fortune, via their professions. As a result of this emphasis on professional success as a means to a better life, we've become a culture that is obsessed with our careers. No other society in the world puts as much value on a person's chosen profession as a way to determine the level of respect they should be given than ours. Don't believe me? I'll show you. Answer the follow three questions with the first thing that comes to mind:

1. Besides their name, when meeting a stranger for the first time, what is one of the first things you would ask them about themselves

2. If you had to stand up and introduce yourself to a room full of strangers, besides your name, what is one of the first things you would tell them about yourself?

3. Name the most successful person you know?

Do you see a pattern in the first two questions? Our culture is conditioned to evaluate one another based on professions. Admit it: The moment we hear what someone does for work, we begin to form an impression about them. But is that really fair? In my private practice, I see hundreds of professionally successful people who are failing miserably in life—and I used to be one of them! (Keep reading and you'll learn more.) In America, our personal identities are so tightly connected to our professions that it directly impacts our ability to be happy in life. Had a bad day at work? Then it's pretty much guaranteed you've had a bad day over all. Work going poorly this month? It's likely your outlook on life is less than stellar for the month as well. In short, we often blame our careers for all that goes wrong in general. But it's the answer to the third question that is most telling…

Did you name someone with significant 'professional' success? When I ask clients this question, the response is always the same. They name a family member, friend, or even a famous person who is successful at what they do for a living – but not necessarily in life as a whole. We put career success on a pedestal in America, often taking a look-the-other-way approach when it comes time to admit their career success is hurting the other areas of their life. How many times have you heard things like:

"It's a shame he's an alcoholic, but he's brilliant in his job."
"It's amazing how hard she works, but that ulcer is going to be the death of her."
"It's too bad that after all his professional success, his marriage failed."

When did 'success' become synonymous with 'professional success' in America? Should we continue to pursue career success at the cost of a satisfying life? Moreover, should we continue to teach other generations that it's okay to fail in life, as long as you are successful professionally?

I believe it's time to change the way we look at careers both for ourselves and for others. That process begins by gaining an individual understanding of what it will take for you to find professional satisfaction, as opposed to chasing career success. The process outlined in this book is designed to make that happen. I hope you will take the time to complete the exercises within these pages so that you can create a personalized definition of career success that will support the ultimate goal: to live a satisfying life.

Don't let your current career reality hold you back from a better future. You can find the satisfaction you want and deserve – but only if you are willing to experience, learn and grow. I hope this book provides that process of enlightenment for you.

Sincerely,

J.T. O'Donnell

Acknowledgments

I can honestly say the research for this book has technically taken most of my life to complete. The coaching techniques shared in these pages reflect what I've learned not only as a coach, but as a person who needed coaching. Therefore, there are quite a few people in my life who need to be recognized for their contributions to this work.

To all of the managers, co-workers, friends and clients I have worked with over the years, I thank you for helping me with my mission. I view the experiences shared with all of you as the equivalent to one very large case study which I've used to fine-tune my approach to coaching.

I thank my father, John, whose passion for career success has had a profound impact on my own. My dad taught me early on that to be successful I needed to be willing to work for what I wanted. My father really does achieve anything he sets his mind to. Moreover, he has always lived his life according to his own set of rules, and he has found success on his own terms. I'm grateful for being able to witness this first hand.

I'd also like to thank my mother, Kay, whose pride and passion for being both a nurse and a mother showed me how important it is to do what you love as well as what you're good at. Her work ethic is rare and admirable. Her energy and vitality are surely as strong as any twenty-year old. Her ability to define and achieve career success on her own terms has made her one of the most professionally satisfied people I know. While most people her age refuse to put any more energy into enhancing their skills to keep up with the times, my mother embraces it. If I could bottle her ability to adapt and grow, I'd be rich!

My brother, John, and my sister, Vicki, have always been extremely supportive of me and my work. It's impossible to count the number of hours they've listened to me talk endlessly about my theories on finding career satisfaction. Their feedback and suggestions throughout this process were invaluable. I can't begin to express how much I cherish my relationship with them and appreciate all they've done to help me.

The arrival of my children, Cassidy and Skylar, made putting my own career into better perspective simple. There is a saying with regard to patience that I love: "You can have it all, you just can't have it all right now." My children have taught me the power of those words.

I must also thank my in-laws, Mike and Sonja, for not only raising a fantastic son, but for being loving and supportive and treating me like their own daughter. I am in the rare position of having a second set of parents who I respect and admire.

Finally, I'd like to thank my husband, Eric, who, from the age of ten, has always known what he wanted to do. To say I've envied his early knowledge of his ideal career path is an understatement. Watching him follow his dream with such focus and patience has been amazing. Keeping it all in perspective and recognizing that no career is perfect, my husband has made having a satisfying career look too easy. I'm still amazed at how he's been able to support me so consistently in my search to find the same kind of career satisfaction. I can honestly say that both this book and my coaching practice would not exist if I didn't have him as my partner in life.

Table of Contents

Part II – The G.L.O.W. Method: Luminate Your Goal 67

Part III – The G.L.O.W. Method: Own Your Actions 81

Part IV – The G.L.O.W. Method: Work It Daily 109

Introduction

The secret of getting ahead is getting started.—Sally Berger

Congratulations! Whether you're just starting out and looking for your first job or you're a workforce veteran looking for a more satisfying career, in choosing to read this book you've taken an important first step towards finding the career success you desire.

This book helps you to:

- Identify your unique definition of career success.
- Understand your personal strengths and preferences and the role they play in achieving your career goals.
- Uncover the thoughts and perceptions that could be holding you back from finding career satisfaction.
- Develop a plan to achieve your personal career goals, both now and in the future.

How is this book different? Unlike other career resources you may have tried, the process outlined in this book takes into account your unique skills, interests and values, enabling each reader to create a truly authentic and realistic plan for career success. The key to your career success lies in the use of the professional methodology and tools included in this book.

Doctors, Lawyers, Accountants and Coaches: Professionals Make A Difference!

Why do people use doctors, lawyers and accountants? Because these individuals are experts in their field and can provide valuable help beyond what the average individual feels they can achieve on their own. The same applies to using a career coach. Career coaches offer personal insight and understanding that most people have trouble evaluating on their own. Moreover, professional career coaches teach valuable tools and resources that can be used both now and in the future.

Unfortunately, the cost of using a good career coach is not always affordable. In fact, some career coaches charge thousands of dollars, making it financially impossible for most people to take advantage of their services. Isn't that ironic? The individuals who need their services the most can't afford them. This is no longer the case. For the first time, a program developed to help individuals identify the right career path for them is being made available to the general public. It's founded on the teachings of **The G.L.O.W. Method**; a four-step process which guides individuals through the complexities of setting and achieving personal goals. In this case, the goal is greater career satisfaction. Let's take a closer look at **The G.L.O.W. Method** - how it was developed and how it will help you find career success on your own terms!

Once Upon A Time…

Every man is the architect of his own fortune.—Sallust

My name is J.T. O'Donnell. I am the creator of **The G.L.O.W. Method** and the author of this book. To really understand why I created **The G.L.O.W. Method** and how I know it will be effective at helping you find greater career satisfaction, I would like to share my story with you.

In 2001, I created my coaching company with the mission of providing valuable yet affordable career development tools. This mission was the culmination of many years of hard work and a determination to change the way humans look at their ability to succeed. What inspired this passion to help others find professional satisfaction?

After earning a B.S. in Engineering Psychology from Tufts University, I was faced with the same task as you: Finding a career I enjoyed that would provide me with all of the things I needed and wanted to be successful and satisfied, both personally and professionally. I had been told all along by the key influencers in my life that a college education would catapult me to success. I followed their advice, so I should have had no problem finding a good, satisfying career, right? Wrong. Unfortunately, several things were working against me. First, I graduated in 1990 at the peak of the recession. After spending thousands of dollars on a first-class education, I was faced with limited entry-level jobs, none of which were appealing. Second, while my university offered a large career center, full of resources to help students identify companies to work for, I felt incapable of utilizing it properly because I did not know how to determine the right career for me. So like many of my friends, I took the path of least resistance and accepted the first job that I could find.

Several years and jobs later, I was feeling unfocused and unfulfilled. The good news was that I was beginning to recognize a pattern. Each job I had taken so far had some interesting traits which had drawn me to it, but soon after the "honeymoon period" of being hired, the newness of the job would wear off and I would find myself unsatisfied and unhappy. As soon as it started to get hard to get out of bed in the morning, I started looking for my next job. My parents were completely distraught. "You are ruining your reputation jumping from job to job," my mom would complain. "You'll never move up the food chain if you keep starting over," my dad would argue. Yet, I secretly disagreed. I actually felt I was doing my employers a favor. I worked hard and gave each job a 150%. It only made sense that I should move on when I felt I couldn't commit myself to the job in the way it deserved. Moreover, at each job I felt I had learned something valuable, even though I hadn't been there twenty years. And, with each job change I made sure the skills acquired in my previous position would be used in my new role. But above all else, I firmly believed that the goal was to find a career I could stay in long-term. What was the point of staying in a career I couldn't see myself doing for the next two, five or even ten years? So, against their wishes, I continued to pursue the "ultimate" job in order to find the "perfect" career. And with each job change I got smarter. I learned to set clear expectations for myself with respect to what I wanted out of my next job. I learned to identify whether the company I worked for had the tools, resources and people I needed to make the most of my strengths and minimize my weaknesses. I learned how to take responsibility for my career success and ways to keep a clear perspective regarding my career's ability to meet my needs. And lastly, I learned what I needed to do on a daily basis to ensure I was always on target with my definition of career success. A decade passed and I had, as they say, "made it." I had proved my parents wrong. My hard work and willingness to move jobs had paid off. I was a senior manager for a prestigious company making a nice six figure income and great benefits. I had stock options, a car allowance and a large expense account.

Life was good, right? Wrong! I was miserable and I couldn't figure out why! I had mastered the ability to achieve my professional goals, yet, personally, I felt extremely unhappy. I was overweight, out of shape and had high blood pressure. I was eating poorly and not taking care of myself. Due to long hours and tons of work, I rarely saw my new husband and spent little time in the new house we had just bought. I would go weeks before I would find the time to call friends and family. I still remember finding a sticky note on my desk from my assistant, letting me know my mother had called and wanted me to return her call right away – the note was a week old. My career was a success, but the rest of my life was a failure. Suddenly it hit me: "Could I even consider my career a success if it was actually the cause of so much personal dissatisfaction?" I'm sure you are thinking this must be the point where I made the radical decision to quit my job and set things straight. Wrong again. Sadly, I opted to ignore my inner dialog and tried to convince myself that I was happy. I reminded myself that I had invested far too much time and energy to give up the career success I had achieved now. It wasn't until a significant and wonderful life-changing event occurred that my desire to change my career became a necessity: The birth of my first child.

A New Perspective On Career

The birth of my daughter had a profound impact on, of all things, my career. I knew I wanted to continue working after she was born, but the idea of working sixty-hour work weeks filled with stress just didn't make sense. Yet, I didn't know what I wanted to do next, and I didn't feel up to the job search process I had so expertly mastered over the years. So I decided to go back to my current job for a bit to see what I thought. That's when fate intervened. I returned to work to find that my company had been purchased by a competitor. I was targeted to help with the merger of our companies and cultures. Usually, a new challenge excited me; this time, however, it was the opposite. The idea of even more work was exactly what I didn't want. I imagined my daughter growing up and me missing it all - her first word, first step and many other firsts that would never come again. Moreover, I couldn't get out of my head the nagging feeling that my lack of presence in her early years would have a negative impact on our relationship. The time had come. Without any back up plan and certainly no idea of what to do next, I quit. It was the most terrifying yet exhilarating thing I've ever done. I spent the next several months in a tug-of-war with my emotions. The fact that I had to quit to get out of my situation made me feel like a failure, yet the empowering feeling of recognizing my need to change and acting upon it was uplifting. The inability to identify the next step in my career was frustrating, yet the opportunity to think about the endless career opportunities was motivating. Some days I would wake up angry with myself for being so unresolved; other days I would awake excited and ready to find a new career.

An Idea Is Born

Whenever you see darkness, there is extraordinary opportunity for the light to burn brighter.—Bono

Determined to improve my situation, I started to look for self-help resources that could shed some light on my situation. I was surprised at how many books there were to help you "find a job," but only a few of them tried to help you determine what career was best for you. I contacted some college students I knew to see if their campus career centers offered any resources in this regard. I learned that just as in my college days, students today were also struggling to determine the right career path for their unique personality, skills and abilities. After many hours of research and not a lot to show for my efforts, I hit an all-time low. Was I taking this too seriously? Was the pursuit of a career that met my life needs just too much to ask for? I was tired of not being able to come up with a personalized career plan that made sense.

Suddenly, it came to me. I look back now and see the irony of the fact that it was only when I was at lowest of the low that my future career became clear. It was as if a light bulb went off in my head. I became so energized by my thoughts that I was bursting with excitement. I realized I needed to develop a systematic way for people to identify and achieve career satisfaction. I had to create a proven method people could learn that would enable them to find new levels of professional success. I didn't want anyone to go through what I was going through, so if there was a way to alleviate some of the anxiety that comes with finding a career path that supports a successful life, I was going to find it. I was on a mission, and there was nothing stopping me.

The G.L.O.W. Method Evolves

I started by becoming a certified life coach. In doing so, I learned exactly why being overly focused on my career success in the past had cost me a happy life. I took what I learned and became my first coaching client. I got organized, built a plan to achieve the balanced life I dreamed of, and went to work on creating the person I wanted to be. No more excuses. I lost weight, got in shape and learned to eat and live well. I made family and friends a priority. But most importantly, I researched and developed a means for individuals to do the self-assessment and development necessary to create their own path to success.

Getting certified as a life coach wasn't my first introduction to coaching. Coaching was always my favorite responsibility as a manager. Having worked in the field of human resources for many years of my corporate life, I loved helping my staff members with professional challenges and had developed a nice set of career coaching tools during that time. Ironic, isn't it? I was great at helping others find professional satisfaction, but had struggled to find it for myself. Thus, I decided to incorporate all the tools I had created for my employees into those I had acquired through my life coaching training - the result was a comprehensive approach to career satisfaction that I knew would be easy for my clients to embrace.

Soon after, I opened my career coaching practice so that I could share this knowledge with as many people as possible. At same time, I wanted to make sure that individuals did not need to spend a fortune on coaching in order to benefit from it. I knew what executive career coaches were charging and that the average person couldn't afford it. So I kept my rates reasonable and built a large coaching practice through word-of-mouth. I used my coaching practice to perfect my tools and solidify a consistent approach to setting and achieve goals that I felt anyone could learn and implement on their own. From my work came **The G.L.O.W. Method** - a simple process for improving professional satisfaction. I'm happy to say that **The G.L.O.W. Method** has helped many people finally understand what it takes to be successful on their own terms. Moreover, I'm proud that a lot of powerful "Ah-ha Moments" have occurred from the use of **The G.L.O.W. Method.**

Ah-ha Moments

Have you ever seen cartoons where the characters have a brilliant idea and a bright light bulb pops up above their heads? Then, they say something like, "Ah-ha! Now I've got it!" In my coaching practice, I refer to the moment when a client has a breakthrough thought or change in perception as an "Ah-ha Moment." I'm hoping this book provides you with many of these important moments. Throughout this book, you will come across text boxes entitled, *Ah-ha Moments*, which contain valuable information I'd like you to consider. As you will learn, these boxes support the first step in **The G.L.O.W. Method**, so I encourage you to take time to reflect on each one. You never know when an important revelation is coming your way!

What Is The G.L.O.W. Method?

When solving problems, dig at the roots instead of just hacking at the leaves. — Anthony J. D'Angelo

Has it ever seemed odd to you that we learn all sorts of important processes as we grow up, (i.e. how to drive a car, balance a checkbook, etc.), yet many of us struggle to learn a process we can use to consistently achieve our goals? Over a lifetime, we learn hundreds of ways to do things. We go to school to learn how to do many tasks, but it doesn't guarantee we'll learn how to be successful.

For years I wondered why this was so hard to figure out on our own. I would ask various individuals who I respected and admired, and they would respond with statements like: "Success is different for everyone, so each person needs to find their own way to be successful." Or, "Success isn't something that can be taught. Each person needs to figure it out for themselves." But the statement that drove me crazy the most was something like this: "Success is what separates unique, special, talented individuals from the rest of the world. You can't learn how to succeed. The ability to succeed is something you're born with."

I pondered these responses but never believed them. I felt these were just statements people used to "explain away" something they didn't understand. Deep down, I felt strongly that just like we learn to tie our shoes or use a computer, there must a way to design and teach humans a simple process to recognize and develop their own best practices for success. Furthermore, I imagined how much disappointment and general frustration in life could be eliminated if people had a way to learn how to be successful on their own terms. I was determined to help others find the peace that comes from knowing how to achieve their goals. Through years of researching and working towards this personal vision, **The G.L.O.W. Method** was created.

Ah-ha Moment: In today's society, it's common practice for people to "explain away" what they can't understand or do for themselves. This is especially true when it comes to personal success. When we can't achieve a goal we see others accomplishing, we often justify or "explain away" how they've managed to be successful where we have not.

For example, seeing individuals who have successfully incorporated exercise into their lifestyle, you've probably heard an observer of their success say, "Well if I had all the time in the world to exercise like she does, I'd be able to work out regularly too." Or, "He's always been athletic. It doesn't take much for him to stay in shape." The same applies to career success. People see someone enjoying true career satisfaction and say, "He probably 'sold his soul' for that job." Or, "She must have known someone in the industry who was able to help her get ahead." Consider this:

- How would you feel if your friends, family or even strangers "explained away" your success?
- What if folks attributed your success to luck, looks, or "being born with it," instead of recognizing your hard work?
- Lastly, ask yourself: Are you guilty of "explaining away" the success of others?

Next time you see someone who is achieving a goal you desire, instead of "explaining away" their success, why not inquire as to how they do it?

The G.L.O.W. Method helps individuals reach new levels of career satisfaction by outlining the four key components to professional achievement. To be successful, you need to G.L.O.W. That means you must:

Gain Perspective
Luminate Your Goal
Own Your Actions
Work It Daily

While many people may be good at one or more of these four key elements, most individuals are not adept at all of them, nor do they know how to improve their ability to execute them consistently and effectively in order to achieve their goal.

The G.L.O.W. Method is extremely helpful because, unlike other self-help tools, it recognizes that no two individuals are the same. It takes into account each person's uniqueness, helping anyone who uses **The G.L.O.W. Method** to customize their approach for better results. Until now, only my private clients benefited from **The G.L.O.W. Method.** I decided to create this book so that I could share my method with the public and help them reach new levels of success as well. My goal is to provide a way for you to experience some of the same results individuals often experience by using a private coach. While good coaches can have a profound impact on a person's life, (one-on-one coaching is always the most powerful), I recognize that many individuals don't have the time or money to take advantage of the consulting services of a professional coach. It's my hope that this book offers a way for anyone who wants to benefit from these practical career insights the opportunity to do so.

G.L.O.W. Your Way To Career Satisfaction

How can **The G.L.O.W. Method** help you with your career? This process will take you through the steps needed to:

- Learn the true definition of "career" as it relates to your life.
- Assess your personal styles and preferences so they can be leveraged in the career selection process.
- Identify your passions and interests and how they impact career satisfaction.
- Pinpoint the best career(s) for you.
- Put together a resumé that supports your efforts.
- Execute a career plan that expands your industry knowledge and job opportunity pipeline.

Sound good? Then let's start by looking at how the definition of "career" has changed in the last three decades and how these changes impact your ability to find career satisfaction.

Yesterday vs. Today

Our dilemma is that we hate change and love it at the same time; what we really want is for things to remain the same but get better.—Sydney J. Harris

Thirty plus years ago, finding a career path was not nearly as complex as it is today. Not only were there far fewer careers to choose from, once you chose a career you were expected to stay in it for the duration of your working days. People were encouraged to work their way up the corporate ladder. Twenty plus years of loyal service meant a retirement package and a gold watch. Changing jobs was taboo. Voluntarily leaving a job with good pay and benefits was career suicide. In other words, once you made your career choice, there was no looking back.

Additionally, people didn't really look at a job as a career. They saw it purely as "work." What's the difference? Work is something you do out of necessity. It puts food on the table and a roof over your head. It's something you have to do, and in the past, it was something that you didn't usually expect to enjoy. Work was not play; you were expected to find personal satisfaction outside of work, via family, friends, hobbies, etc. For better or worse, (and I think it's for the better), those days are gone. Our quality of life has improved, and while we still need to work, (i.e. put food on the table and a roof over our heads), we are lucky enough to be able to choose from an endless array of career choices to do so. More importantly, we now have the opportunity to find a career path that provides personal satisfaction as well. In addition to doing a job we are good at, we can do a job we enjoy. And, should we no longer enjoy a career, we are not forced to live with our choice for the duration of our working years. Changing jobs is no longer the exception; it is the norm. Thanks to the incredible rate of change in our world, the state of business has been dramatically altered. Companies come and go. (Remember the technology boom of the 90's?). New industries are being created with each innovation. Technology improves year-over-year, and job descriptions seem to evolve daily.

Whether we want to or not, these changes force us to constantly reevaluate our career choices and their ability to meet our wants and needs both now and in the future. Ironically, this career evolution is causing a lot of problems. In fact, depending on which survey you read, anywhere from 50-70+% of the American workforce claims to be dissatisfied with their careers and actively looking for a better job.

What does this mean? Having so many career options as well as a multitude of elements to consider with respect to professional satisfaction does have its drawbacks. Suddenly, instead of just finding a job that covers our basic needs, we must consider so much more:

- How do I pick a career I will enjoy?
- How can I make best use of my unique skills and interests to ensure my success?

- How do I make sure I'm learning skills I can use in the future?
- How do I know a particular job will work well with the other areas of my life (i.e. finances, family, etc.)?
- When and how should I change careers when I recognize the one I'm in is no longer working for me?

And to make matters worse, some of the answers to these questions will change over time. In particular, you will find your career needs shifting as you pass through each of the three phases of your career.

Three Career Phases

Many of my clients are surprised to hear me refer to them as being in a particular "phase" with respect to their career. However, through my coaching practice, I have found that there are three distinct stages an individual goes through in the lifecycle of their career. With the average person working more than forty years in a lifetime, it only makes sense that the role our careers play in our life would change during that time. Let's look at each phase.

Phase I: Skill & Preference Development

This initial phase represents the first ten to fifteen years of our career. During this time, we are just starting out in the working world and are most likely out on our own for the first time in our adult lives. Thus, while we do try to find a career we enjoy, we are also driven by the desire to earn an income and develop a lifestyle separate from our parents or guardians. The main goal for most individuals during this phase is paying the bills while building our dreams for the future. Unfortunately, many people are so preoccupied with this goal that they don't see the importance of picking a career path that suits them for the long-term. Any reasonable job with decent benefits and perks is considered a good move. Unfortunately, this lack of planning and development with respect to a person's personal strengths and interests often leads to bigger challenges in the subsequent phases.

Phase II: Lifestyle Maintenance & Personal Growth

The second phase represents the fifteen to twenty-five year marks of career. By now, personal life experiences have started to transform us. Marriage, children and buying a home are often events that take place during this phase, if they haven't already. These major changes have a profound impact on our perception of career. At the same time, we have also established our lifestyle with respect to material elements and have generally reached a financial level that unchanged would at least be able to keep us independent, healthy and relatively happy. Here's the problem: In order to get to this point, many individuals recognize that they have chosen career paths that have suited them financially but do not provide the kind of long-term satisfaction, stimulation and overall personal happiness they want. In other words, they don't enjoy what they do and can't imagine doing it for the remainder of their working life. This becomes even more disconcerting because the ability to "start over" and choose a career they truly love appears impossible due to the financial constraints they have created. I refer to this as the "Golden Handcuff Effect" – and when feeling held hostage in this manner, many people become depressed and irritable. Moreover, if left unsolved, their career dissatisfaction can dramatically affect other areas of their life. Health may deteriorate and relationships may become strained. The prospect of spending the next twenty years doing something unfulfilling has a truly negative impact on a person's ability to be happy in the final phase of their career. Thus, the possibility of becoming unhappy with life in general is real.

Phase III: Wisdom, Balance & Fulfillment

In the final phase, individuals should be spending the last twenty years finding great personal satisfaction from their careers. A foundation has been built and the rewards are to be reaped. People should be sitting in a position of knowledge and power that enables them to be creative and forth giving with their career wisdom. People in this phase get great satisfaction out of their career but don't need to work more than forty hours a week to do it. In fact, many people who successfully reach this phase are able to get exactly what they need from their career on a limited time schedule. They recognize that career is only one element of their life and, therefore, have not placed too much responsibility or value on their career with regard to their overall happiness. Career should be more about personal growth and fulfillment at this stage. Having fun and loving what you do are important elements here. Will you have the occasional bad day in Phase III? Of course you will, but, overall, your career will have become a great source of pleasure and security.

Unfortunately, many people never experience Phase III in the way I have described it above. All too often, I hear stories of people who spent those years toiling away in a job they despised. To console themselves, they often found other outlets—some good, some bad—but none strong enough to offset the dissatisfaction felt on the job. It pains me to hear stories of people who have created such stressful, unhappy lives as a result of their career that they become sick or die, usually right when they are getting ready to finally retire! There is such irony in the idea that someone could work so hard in a job they hate just to have the goal of finding happiness in their retirement years ripped away. Who wants to spend their retirement days nursing their bad health or regretting the relationships that they ruined along the way?

This can be the result of not finding the kind of career satisfaction you want and deserve. If you are reading this book, then no doubt you've come to recognize you don't want this to happen to you.

Do the Right Thing Now...Or Pay Later

What can be learned from the three career phases? Take the time in Phase I to really hone in on what is important to you. Identify your unique strengths and interests and use them to find the best career options for you. For those of you who are already in Phase II and are unhappy, don't worry. You can make career changes that will transform your situation and help you find career happiness. You'll just need to be ready to do a little extra work and soul searching to help you improve your future. Lastly, if you are in Phase III, we can even help you! You'll need to make some pretty profound changes with respect to how you view your life and the role your career plays in it, but, if you are willing, you can find the career happiness you want and deserve. No matter what phase you are in, you can improve your career situation.

What You'll Need

The beginning is the most important part of any work.—Plato

Before we begin, I suggest you get a spiral bound notebook. You'll be completing many important exercises as you go through this book and will want to keep your answers someplace handy. You'll be referring back to these answers often, so having them in a bound book is the best way to keep them together. Keeping a hard copy will enable you to access your work anytime you want. But most importantly, the act of physically writing your answers will help you clarify your thoughts and make measurable progress. In short, your notebook is an important part of the effective execution of this methodology. Once you have your notebook, you're ready to move on.

PART I

THE G.L.O.W. METHOD: Gain Perspective

STEP #1: Gain Perspective

We all live with the objective of being happy; our lives are all different and yet the same.—Anne Frank

Gaining perspective simply means you need to take a step back and assess yourself and your situation. Using various tools to help you, you will take an inventory of your self knowledge to evaluate your current values, preferences and interests. This information is used to uncover roadblocks and create customized plans for achieving success. In gaining perspective of yourself and your situation, you are able to develop an approach to your goal that is right for you. No two people are the same. Therefore, no two people should focus on a goal in the same way. This is especially true for career goals. Each of us likes to do different things and wants different results from our careers. We should never try to copy or mimic someone else's career plan, because it just won't be as effective as the one we create for ourselves. That said, to begin the process of gaining perspective, you must first assess if your career is really the area of your life right now that needs the most attention.

Are You Out Of Balance?

Minds are like parachutes—they only function when open.—Thomas Dewey

When clients first come to me, it's usually because they feel certain that in order to find greater happiness in life they need to focus on improving their career. Yet, I always begin by having them complete the Life Balance Grid. This is a grid I designed to show visually how satisfied clients are with their life by breaking down their satisfaction in to eight key areas. The grid looks like this:

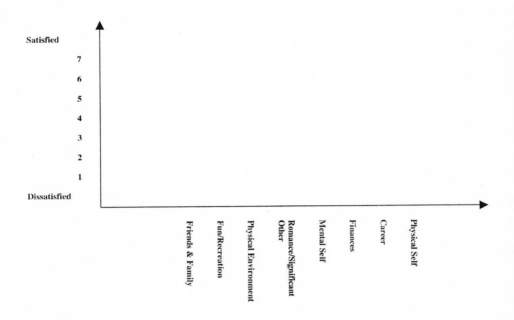

Completing The Life Balance Grid

It's time for you to complete the Life Balance Grid for yourself. With 1 being "very dissatisfied" to 7 being "very satisfied," use the grid above to graph your current satisfaction level in the eight key areas of life. Connect the dots to look at your results. Do you have a straight line? Do you have peaks and valleys? What do the results say about your current ability to keep all the key areas of your life at satisfactory levels? How does one area impact another? More importantly, which area(s) is the lowest on your grid? Is it *career*? If not, then why aren't you choosing the lowest scoring area(s) on your grid to focus on first?

As a coach, I've generally found the lowest point on a person's grid is the area of life which should be focused on first. While you may be interested in improving your career, if it isn't the lowest point on your grid, it just might not be the right time for you to change it. Why? In my experience, the clients who were the most committed to succeed were the ones who were focused on improving the area to which they gave the lowest satisfaction ranking. In other words, the best chance you have for setting and achieving a personal goal right now is by selecting a goal that would improve the key area you are least satisfied with. In fact, I can tell you from experience that focusing on the lowest scoring area on your grid can also serve to improve the other areas of your life as well. These eight areas are interdependent upon one another. While each one acts independently, they still impact one another.

To put it simply, you need to recognize whether or not another area of your life needs attention over your career. Are you faulting your job for your dissatisfaction when another area is actually to blame? Let me share with you an example of how easy it is to confuse the need to improve one area of your life with the need to improve your career.

MISTAKE #1 – Focusing On *Career* Instead Of *Physical Self*

A client, Sean, came to me extremely distraught over his job. He hated going to work everyday and was so depressed about his lack of interest in work that it was beginning to affect his relationship with his spouse and other family members. I recall him saying, "I'm so angry about my work situation that I find myself snapping at my love ones for no reason." His spouse also confided in me that he was drinking several or more alcoholic beverages each night just so he could relax. Given the situation as described, I'm sure most of us would agree that this client's lowest point on the Life Balance Grid would be *career*. Yet to my surprise, when he completed the grid, there was one key area that ranked lower! It was *physical self*. I questioned my client in detail as to why he felt this area was in even worse shape than his career. He confided in me that he was extremely unhappy with his physical appearance. He had gained quite a bit of weight since his younger days, and he didn't feel he looked his personal best. I inquired as to how his low self-esteem regarding his appearance was impacting his work. He admitted that he didn't feel confident because he didn't think he "looked the part" of someone who was smart and important. He felt he didn't deserve any respect from his co-workers and managers because he didn't "look" capable of taking good care of himself. Additionally, when I asked about his *mental self* rating, (which had almost as low as *physical self*), he explained that lately he wasn't feeling as "smart" as other people and was beginning to question his intellect. Again, I inquired about this perception of his mental self's impact on his career. He explained that, in particular, he was feeling inferior to his co-workers and managers. He said there were many questions he had about his work, but he was afraid and embarrassed to ask these questions for fear he would look incapable of doing his job. When I asked my client why he wasn't choosing to focus on his physical self first, he explained that he felt too depressed and drained to put any energy into getting in shape. He was convinced that if he could find a new job, he would be happier and thus would find the energy and inspiration to start working out.

Upon learning this valuable information about my client, I was able to pose a simple question to him: "If we could improve your physical appearance, do you think you would be happier at your current job?" He replied, "Well of course." So I followed up with a final question, "What if we find you a new job and you still don't improve your physical appearance, is it possible you will feel inferior and eventually be unhappy in that job too?" Upon a long moment of reflection, my client looked at me and admitted that yes, it was highly possible that changing jobs could still land him right back where he was today. We talked some more, and it slowly became clear to him that his goal was not to improve his career, but rather to improve his physical self. Just finding a new job was not going to solve my client's problem.

We refocused my client's goal on getting in shape and feeling better about his looks. My client started exercising and set a weight loss goal for himself which he achieved in just two months. It's no surprise that his confidence at work soared and his fear of "looking inadequate" disappeared. Not only did his satisfaction with his physical self improve, but *mental self* and *career* got a big boost on his Life Balance Grid as well.

What would have happened if I had let my client continue to believe that his career was the source of his unhappiness? Do you think he would have addressed his issues with his physical self? Can you imagine how my client would have felt if he had invested all his time in improving his career and it still didn't make him feel any better?

Take time now to assess the lowest area on your Life Balance Grid and see if setting a goal to improve it might have positive affects on other key areas of your life as well. Once you've identified an area of life you'd like to make better, you can begin to outline the process for setting an achievable goal for it. The good news is that while this book focuses on using The G.L.O.W. Method to help improve career satisfaction, you can still review the method and use many of the tools in this book to help improve satisfaction in any of the other key areas of life. So please, keep reading!

Is Your Focus Misguided?

More people would learn from their mistakes if they weren't so busy denying them.
—Harold J. Smith

As I mentioned earlier, I often have clients approach me with the desire to change careers, but upon completing the Life Balance Grid, it becomes clear they need to focus on another key area of life first. There are several common situations in which people mistakenly try to improve their life via their career, when they should actually be focusing their efforts on something else. I already shared with you MIS-TAKE #1: Convincing yourself that if you found a better career, you would be able to take better care of yourself. So many times clients tell me that if they weren't so stressed out and actually enjoyed their job, they would find the motivation to eat better, get in shape, quit smoking, etc... Yet, this just isn't the case. Only when you find a way to improve your physical self and stop using one of the other areas of life as an excuse will your chances for long-term happiness be possible. Let's face it, our lives are always changing. Therefore, you must find a way to be successful in each area of life separately. As I mentioned earlier, while the eight key areas of life are interrelated, they are also independent of one another. This means that you must find a way to maintain happiness in each area without relying on another area to do so. I have identified four additional mistakes people often make where their desire to improve career is misguided.

MISTAKE #2 – Focusing On *Career* Instead Of *Finances* Or *Physical Surroundings*

Too many people spend money they haven't earned to buy things they don't want to impress people they don't like.—Will Rogers

Often clients rank finances as low if not lower than career. They usually tell me they are unhappy with their income level, and that they blame their career situation. Moreover, many of these same people tell me their physical surroundings are okay, but that they would like the ability to buy more things. Ironically, it's not the career that's causing the problem, it's their spending habits! This may seem obvious to you, but let me share with you an example that you may find yourself guilty of.

I had a client, Mike, who was earning a great living as a manager for a prestigious Fortune 500 company. Unfortunately, he was miserable. When he came to me, he was experiencing anxiety attacks and difficulty sleeping. We discussed his situation, and he explained that his goal was to get promoted at work. I asked his reasoning behind this goal and he responded by saying: "If I could get this promotion, I will get a $10,000 raise. I can then use this money to outsource some of the chores I need to do around the house, like mowing the lawn and many of the other projects that come with maintaining my 4,000 square foot home. That way, I can free up more time to spend with my wife and two children." I had one question for him. "How much more time will you be spending on the job as a result of the promotion?" He thought about it for a while and finally admitted, "Probably at least ten extra hours each week." My next question was even simpler: "So will the raise really make your life better?" It was immediately apparent to my client that his goal was completely off base. The trade-off was terrible. My client and I went back to basics and looked at how he had been viewing the purpose of his career. Like many individuals, he realized that he had been using his career as the main way to improve his finances and physical surroundings. All of his happiness in these two key areas of life was completely dependent on his career.

Can you imagine the pressure he felt with regard to career success? For him, a big salary was a must. Therefore, keeping the job he had so the income level could be maintained was an overwhelming priority. Unfortunately, in viewing his career this way, it left no room for him to discover his true passions and to follow a career path that could give him great personal satisfaction.

Now certainly the idea of picking and staying with a career solely on the ability to make money might make sense initially. But look where my client was as a result? He had everything he could want including a big house, a fancy car; yet he was miserable. We know money doesn't buy happiness. We also know that being a slave to money can make you very unhappy. My client was holding himself to his current career because he felt he had to maintain his income level in order to keep the lifestyle he and his family enjoyed. I'm happy to say that my client was quick to realize that if he kept up this view of career and its relation to his finances and physical surroundings, many other areas of his life would suffer. We discussed the lack of time he was able to spend with his family and wife and the impact that could have on his future relationships with them. We also discussed the effect his career unhappiness would have eventually on his physical and mental health.

What kind of toll would the stress have on him? In short, my client was able to see that the so-called "success" he thought he had been experiencing with regard to his career so far was no success at all. My client and his spouse immediately went to work on a plan for them to become financially less-dependent upon his career. They assessed their lifestyle and pared down their expenses. They reevaluated what was important and refocused their priorities. They even built up a savings account they could draw upon in the event my client wanted to quit his job and change careers. Guess what happened? My client began to enjoy his job again! Suddenly, the pressure was lifted, and he was able to focus on his work and the elements of it that gave him satisfaction. He became more productive and happy on the job. He no longer worked in fear of losing the job he thought he needed to be happy. As a result, he started to make innovative changes that were well received by his employer. In fact, several months later, he was even offered the promotion he had so desperately wanted to obtain when we first met. What did he do? Did I advise him not to take it? No. By now, he had figured out how to be successful in his career without hurting the other areas of his life. He accepted the promotion but only on the condition that he would maintain the same flexible work schedule he had recently created for himself. His employer was happy to oblige, and he was happy to use the increase in his salary to take his family on vacation!

I frequently see clients make the mistake of thinking that the only way to improve their financial situation or physical surroundings is through the money they earn in their career. This puts a lot of weight on the success of your career. To avoid this mistake, I encourage you to make sure you do the following:

1) Assess your goals for finances and physical surroundings. Are they too much at the moment? Do your desires for these areas put undo pressure on your career?
2) What can you do to make your financial and physical surroundings success separate from your career? How can you earn money in a non-traditional way to supplement your career earnings? How can you save money for your own safety fund in the event you want to change careers?

By eliminating the total dependency of your financial and physical surroundings success upon your career, you will immediately see greater satisfaction in all three areas.

MISTAKE #3 – Putting *Career* Before *Family/Friends & Romance/Significant Other*

Having been personally guilty of this mistake for several years, I find this one very important. I was lucky enough to have had a life experience to help me recognize my error. But many people never understand the negative impact of putting work before relationships. Let me share another client story with you.

Lara came to me suffering from what she believed was acute career stress. Lara was a very successful salesperson. She earned an incredible six-figure income and was able to buy herself whatever she wanted. She was beautifully dressed with perfect hair, make-up and nails, and her jewelry was exquisite. She drove a BMW and owned her own townhouse. To the outside world, Lara was a big success. Unfortunately, what Lara didn't share with the outside world was the anxiety she was feeling. Lara couldn't sleep for more than three hours at a time. She would wake up and find her mind racing about work. Lara suspected she must be unhappy in her career. "It's keeping me up at night. I like what I do, but lately, I feel sad and tired all the time. On the weekends, when I have some time off, I find myself lying in bed all day trying to get some rest. It's getting harder and harder to find ways to feel happy or excited. Something must be wrong with me." My first question to Lara was, "How many hours do you work each week?" Lara explained that she was always working. Her entire life was based around work. When she went out to eat, it was a business dinner. When she entertained in her home, it was co-workers who came over. When she went away, it was a business meeting. More importantly, Lara even admitted that she was so busy that she rarely had time to see her family and friends. Although her parents and siblings lived just forty minutes away, she only saw them at holidays.

I asked Lara to explain why she put so much into her career. Lara stated that she had always felt out of place and not very special as a kid. "I was always trying to be part of the "in crowd," but I never really felt like people respected me. I wasn't particularly good at anything, and I never really found my place. It wasn't until I graduated from college and started working that I realized I was a good at selling. My first boss said I was "a natural," and I got a lot of praise and respect for my abilities. I quickly climbed the ranks and was doing much better in my career than most of my friends. For the first time, I felt like I was good at something. I really blossomed as a person. Even my family and friends commented on my change in confidence. Since then, I've kept working hard so that I can continue to reach my professional and financial goals." Next, I asked Lara if she had any desire to have someone special in her life. She said, "Yes, but so far, no one has been able to understand my work schedule. Besides, I just don't have time to date." Last, I asked Lara how in touch she felt with her family and friends. For example, did she know what was going on in their lives? She answered with, "I know they are okay, they would call me if anything was really wrong. Besides, they know if they truly need me, they can call me. It's an unwritten rule we have."

After much discussion, I could see that being indirect wasn't going to work with Lara because she saw her situation as completely normal. She had wanted me to determine why her career was giving her so much anxiety, so I explained to Lara that she was using her career as her main source of identity. In other words, she was assessing her personal self-worth completely by her career success. Clients often use their career as their main source of happiness and validation, and, in doing so, put too much pressure on their career. Lara thought that by being a big success in her career, she would feel like a success as a person overall. I knew her anxiety was from her fear of losing her career success. If she couldn't remain the best at her career, then she couldn't keep on believing she was "special." Unfortunately, Lara couldn't see that her so called career success was costing her success in other areas of her life. So I asked Lara the toughest question of all: Why she felt her career was more important than her family, friends and relationships. She answered angrily, "My career is not more important than my family and friends, it just requires more time from me. They understand that. They know what it takes to be successful. They realize I must work like this. And I don't need someone in my life who can't understand the importance of my career!" I knew I had hurt Lara's feelings, but as a coach, it's my job to deliver the hard news. So I asked her several more tough questions such as, "Lara, is working so much that you can't make time for family and friends really being successful in your eyes? Does putting your career before people who love you really make the most sense to you? Can you honestly call yourself a good family member and friend? Would you want to be in a relationship with someone who valued work more than you?" Lara was so upset with what I asked that we had to end our session. I knew she was questioning everything she had worked so hard to achieve. For the first time, she was looking at the life she had created for herself and asking, "Am I actually a failure?"

By our next session, Lara had reflected on what I'd said. She admitted that while it hurt to hear, she really always knew that what she was doing wasn't right. In fact, she even recognized that some of the anxiety she had been feeling was from the knowledge that she was ignoring some very important people in her life. "I knew the lifestyle I was working so hard to achieve was very self-centered. But it just felt so good in the beginning to feel important and valued, that I wanted to hold on to that feeling. I realize now that I want to be a well-rounded person, and that means giving my relationships with my family and friends more attention. I miss spending time with them. I realized I was so sad on the weekends because I was alone. I see now that I need to be with the people I love and who love me." By redefining her self-worth based on her ability to balance her life and put her priorities in order, Lara was able to let go of her "power career" and still feel respected. Lara cut back her hours and stopped putting so much time into her career. To her surprise, she was still valued and successful on the job. In fact, several co-workers and her manager confided in her that she seemed to be much more "human" and "in touch" than before. Lara was even more shocked to find out that the reason senior management had never considered her for a management role in the past was because she seemed too focused on her own success and, therefore, wouldn't be good at helping others. Lara's change of focus showed her softer side. For the first time, her manager could see she cared about others. As she rebuilt her relationships with her family and friends, she found out just how out of touch she had been. Lara became much happier at work. She was no longer drained. Her weekends were busy spending time with family and friends. I'm happy to say that Lara even met someone special. Her new outlook on her career had finally given her time to date! Lara's growth as a person also took her to new heights in her career. She was promoted to manager one year later, where she mentors other salespeople on how to be successful, both personally and professionally!

Don't make the mistake of using your career as your main identifier as a person. Being a "work-o-holic" is not something to be proud of. Moreover, don't try to convince yourself that if you get ahead now, you'll have more time to spend with your family and friends. Sacrificing your most important relationships, even temporarily, can have adverse affects. What if one of your closest relatives or friends died today? Would you be remorse in having put your relationship with them on the back burner while you worked to "make it" professionally? A manager I worked with once gave me a great piece of advice. She said: "Keep your family and friends close because your career can't sit with you at the Thanksgiving table!"

MISTAKE #4 – When *Career* Is Responsible For *Mental Self*

Another classic scenario I encounter frequently in my coaching practice is the client who gets "bored easily" on the job.

Derek was a very bright guy. He was considered a wise old soul amongst his friends. When Derek came to me, he was on his fourth career since graduating from college seven years earlier. Derek was very depressed. In his words, "I just can't seem to find a career that keeps me interested. I find something and dive into it full force, but usually after six months to a year, I'm so bored, I have trouble getting myself out of bed in the morning." Of course, Derek kept his unhappiness to himself. None of his friends or family knew of his boredom. Derek had become acceptant of his urge to change careers so he kept his expenses low and his savings in check, just so he could quit at any time. "I end up starting over so much that I don't really ever get to the point in any career where the financial rewards improve." Derek wanted to be able to build his financial security, but he was too afraid that he would get "locked into a career" just because of the income level it afforded. "I see so many of my friends held hostage to their careers because of the bills they've amassed," commented Derek, "I just won't do that to myself."

Derek was hoping I could help him find a single career he could stay with long-term. Unfortunately, I knew that wouldn't be the case. I began by asking Derek to describe what he felt a career had to offer for him to be truly happy. Derek answered, "I want a career that stimulates me mentally. It should challenge me and keep me busy. I want to be learning as much as I can, but I want the learning to be exciting. It has to peak my interest." Next, I asked Derek to explain in detail what his life was like when he started a new job. He stated, "It's great. It's like an adrenaline rush. I throw myself into my work and focus on it all day. I find myself working extra hours and trying to get as much knowledge about it as I can. Sometimes, I'm so in to it, I forget to eat! It takes over my life." Upon further discussion, I asked Derek to describe how the other areas of his life are affected during these time periods. He responded, "Well, I know I tend to ignore a lot of things. I don't exercise much or spend any time on leisure activities, and I realize I spend less time with family and friends, but it's only because I'm so inspired. Besides, my experience shows that soon my excitement for the job will be gone and I will have more time to pay attention to those areas."

It was time to help Derek see how his approach to his career was his own problem. I asked him, "Why must your career be your only outlet for mental stimulation?" His answer was, "Because that's what a career is for." My next question was, "Why can't you find the same challenge and excitement outside of work?" To this, he said, "I like to relax outside of work. I don't want to be mentally challenged. I like to rest." I questioned him further, "Is it possible you are so tired from straining your brain at work that you don't have any energy to use your mind outside of work?" Derek admitted this was possible. "I guess I just always wanted to work my brain on the job, and then take a rest. But I guess I could always find ways to challenge myself through other means." I proposed a new concept for Derek: "In your next career, why not try pacing yourself and paying attention to the other areas of your life? Your goal shouldn't be total submersion into your career but rather an attempt at balancing all the areas of your life by giving them equal attention. Moreover, finding a hobby that challenges you mentally could also help you recognize the value in a job that isn't so intellectually that it causes you to burn out." Derek saw the merit of my suggestion, but admitted he thought he would miss the adrenaline rush that throwing himself into a new job provided. We discussed how he could find that excitement in other ways: By exploring the other areas of his life and how he could challenge himself in each one. Derek decided he would stay in his current job and try creating greater balance in his life. By sticking with a job he already knew well, he was able to spend less time at work and more time developing a hobby. Ironically, Derek found he loved working with his hands and started taking art classes. He became so involved in this hobby (what a surprise!) that he eventually was able to sell some of his work. Now, Derek uses both his career and his hobbies to stimulate his brain. He no longer finds himself bored, since he now has several outlets which challenge him mentally.

Expecting your career to provide you with all the mental stimulation and growth you want is unrealistic. You will find yourself riding way too many highs and lows with respect to your good and bad days on the job. No matter how much work you do to find a career path that's best for you, you will not be able to escape the fact that, at times, your career will have its boring periods. When this occurs, you must find ways to stimulate your brain outside of work. It will be your ability to look forward to this stimulation that will help you get through the occasionally slow periods of your career. Give this a try before you decide to give up your current career altogether. Do this especially if your current career meets most of your criterion for career happiness. (You'll have an opportunity to assess this later on in the book.)

MISTAKE #5 – When *Career* Doubles As *Fun & Recreation*

In the same way some people expect their career to be their main source of mental growth and stimulation, some also make career their only outlet for fun and creativity.

Erin was happy with her career. As a small business owner, she loved the freedom and creativity she had in setting her own goals. In Erin's own words, "I determine how successful I want to be. It's so exciting to find new ways to improve sales and grow my business." So why was Erin coming to see me? Erin was starting to feel some depression and was concerned that it might be related to her work. She explained: "I'm starting to lose interest in my company. I'm questioning what I'm doing. I'm earning a good living for my family and providing an important service to my clients, but something inside me is telling me it is no longer enough. I feel terribly guilty for thinking this way, but I can't seem to get myself out of this funk. I don't have as much enthusiasm for the work as I did. It's like all the best ideas have already come out of me." Erin said she had tried taking a vacation or two, but they only helped to temporarily improve her mood. While Erin's problem was unclear to her, it was obvious to me. I started my questioning by asking her to describe what she did in her free time. "Free time? I don't like to have free time," said Erin. "I like to be productive. I usually catch up on my industry reading for the business or try some brainstorming exercises to help me come up with some new strategies. My work is great in that it is something I can do in my free time." I went on and asked Erin, "Tell me some of your hobbies outside of work?" She sat for at least two minutes before saying, "Well I love to sew and I like seeing plays, but there isn't much time to do either of those things." I responded with, "Why not?" To which Erin admitted that she was too busy with work. My next question was simple, "When was the last time you researched and pursued a new hobby?" Erin laughed and said quite honestly, "I don't remember." I asked Erin to tell me why she thought she didn't pursue any hobbies. She pondered the question and finally concluded that she felt hobbies weren't 'productive.' "I'd rather do something of value," she commented. To this I responded, "Isn't pursuing a hobby in which you use your brain and body in a different method than usual being productive? Can't you identify a hobby that forces you to think outside the box and challenge yourself in ways that your career can't?" Erin agreed this was possible, but that she would still feel she was being frivolous with her time. So I asked her, "What if a hobby helped you improve your mind and body so that you could give more back to your career?" Erin's interest was peaked by this question. "What if you used your hobby as a way to see the world differently, ultimately, helping you to be more creative on the job, wouldn't that be of value to you?" Erin agreed that this concept definitely made sense. "I never really looked at hobbies as important, but now I can see your point."

We decided to start focusing on Erin's passions and interests to see if we could identify a new hobby. Erin realized that she was really into fitness. She decided to learn how to rock climb. She started taking classes and even joined a club. After her first real climb, she called to tell me how invigorating it had been. "I'm having so much fun, just like when I started up my business. My energy level is back." Erin realized that all the time and energy she had put into her business had afforded her the opportunity to pull back a bit and let it run at a steady pace so that she could spend a some time pursuing her new passion. She took several rock climbing vacations and had made many new friends. But best of all, Erin's new hobby was having profound effects on her business. "My creativity is at an all time high. I'm identifying all sorts of new services to offer. I never realized how much I had been limiting my customers, but getting out, meeting new people, and trying new things has opened my eyes once again to the endless possibilities in my business. I'm so thankful to have realigned my priorities and recognized the need for hobbies."

Hobbies provide a valuable resource for us in life. We learn from hobbies, we gain satisfaction from hobbies. Fun and recreation are an integral part of a successful life. Trying too hard to make fun and recreation be "productive" can have a negative impact on your life balance. Hobbies are meant to be enjoyed. Ironically, when people pay attention to the need for fun and recreation, they often get the added benefit of producing some wonderful life altering results. In fact, toward the end of this book, I will discuss a huge trend in career development that involves the use of hobbies as a way to build and transition to a new career.

In summary, it is imperative you learn to separate the eight key areas of life from one another. Using your career to improve another area may offer some short-term satisfaction, but it will not provide long-term happiness. That said, once certain you are focusing on your career for the right reasons, you can move on and begin identifying the role career plays in the grand scheme of your deepest beliefs, a.k.a. your Core Values.

Core Values: What Do You Care About Most?

As we saw from the Life Balance Grid, your career is just one of eight key areas in your life. Collectively, we refer to these eight elements as your "Core Values." To recap, they are as follows:

Physical Self
Career
Finances
Mental Self
Romance/Significant Other
Physical Surroundings
Fun/Recreation
Family & Friends

Ranking Your Core Values

In your notebook, take a moment to rank the eight key areas of life in order of value. In your opinion, which is most important? What should be taken care of first, second, third, etc.? Continue with your list until you have ranked them all. Where did career fall on your list? Was it first, last or somewhere in the middle? Identifying where career falls in your priority order is very important because it will help to determine what careers work with your Core Values, not against them.

Ah-ha Moment: Do you think everyone should have the eight key areas of life ranked the same way? Of course not! One thing that makes each person unique is the way in which they prioritize their values. Rarely do two people rank these eight areas in the exact same order.

That said, it's important to remember there is no such thing as a "right" order. Each person must prioritize the eight key areas of life based on their own wants and needs, not someone else's. So the next time you encounter someone who has different priorities than yours, remember: you don't need their approval, and they don't need yours. Live your lives based on your own priorities, just respect each other's right to be different!

Success Statements

A man is a success if he gets up in the morning and gets to bed at night, and in between he does what he wants to do.—Bob Dylan

Now that you have prioritized your Core Values, it's time to write a Success Statement for each one. A Success Statement is simply a definition that describes what you wish to achieve in that area of life. For each one, you should write a brief summary that outlines what you believe constitutes success for that element.

In your notebook, take a moment now to write your Success Statements.

Success Statements: Yours vs. Someone Else's

Happiness does not come from doing what you want, but wanting what you do. — Unknown

Writing down your goals, a.k.a. your Success Statements, is only half the battle. We still need to confirm that your goals are truly your own. You might be thinking, "Well of course they're mine, I just wrote them!" Yet, many people don't realize what they've just written down are actually not their own definitions of success, but those of others. How is that possible? As we grow up, we are influenced by many people. Parents, teachers, friends and lots of other well-intentioned individuals share their personal definitions of success in an effort to help us. Unfortunately, many people mistakenly end up adopting these definitions of success as their own, without first validating them to confirm they are actually in sync with their Core Values. This can have a devastating effect on a person's ability to find a truly satisfying career path. Let's look at a real-life example.

Betsy was a young college graduate from a prestigious Ivy League school. She had always been a straight-A student and was involved in all sorts of extracurricular activities. Upon graduation from her university, she spent a year working for a non-profit organization tutoring under-privileged children. At the end of her year-long commitment, she was offered and accepted a job with a top consulting firm. After two years with the consulting firm, she was a big success and had the opportunity to move on to the next level in the organization. Betsy came to me at this point, unhappy and confused. She felt she hadn't found her, "true calling" and was, "very unhappy and unmotivated" in her current position. Additionally, she felt, "angry and embarrassed" with herself for not being happy. She realized she had a dream job and a great salary that any number of young professionals her age would love to have. Moreover, she was good at her job and found it easy to be successful at it. When I asked her if she simply wanted to go back to non-profit work, she replied, "no." She said the work she had done in the past was "rewarding, but not enough of a challenge." She was at a complete loss of what to do.

I started by having Betsy create Success Statements for each key area. After much contemplation, Betsy admitted she was having a lot of trouble writing a Success Statement for career. So I began by asking her what she felt had been driving her career success so far. She said she felt obligated to make her parents proud of her, and so she had tried to create a career direction they would approve of. I then asked if she felt her parents had similar definitions of career success. She laughed and said, "Oh no! They're completely different people!" Further discussion revealed that Betsy's father was a successful business executive who defined career success as financial wealth from his career efforts. Betsy's mother, on the other hand, had a PhD and believed career success involved using your abilities to make a large impact on society. Do you see how Betsy might be confused? Up to this point, Betsy had not created a definition of career success for herself. Instead, she had tried being successful by using her parents' definitions of career success. I'm sure this made them quite proud, but no wonder she felt unfulfilled! I pointed out to Betsy that she was defining her career success by her parents' definitions, not her own. More importantly, her parents had such opposite views of career success; it was no wonder it was proving impossible for Betsy to be happy. Pleasing one parent only served to disappoint another. Lastly, I asked Betsy to think about each of her parent's career success and asked her if she admired or desired the kind of success either one of them had achieved. She thought about it for a while. It was suddenly apparent that Betsy was having an Ah-ha Moment. At last, Betsy realized she didn't want the career success either of her parents had achieved. Betsy finally understood that if she was going to find happiness with regard to her career, it was time for her to create her own Success Statement and make it happen. "It's like a weight has been lifted off of me," Betsy commented. "I never realized I was trying so hard to please my parents, when I didn't even want what they had. I don't like disappointing them, but it's my life, and I can't spend it being unhappy. I know that if I can find my own version of career success and achieve it, my parents will be proud of me. They always tell me they want me to be happy, I guess now it's time to see if they mean it."

Betsy decided that what she really wanted at this phase of her career was to find work in a foreign country. She recognized the opportunity to travel and live somewhere else would be less attractive to her when she decided to settle down and have children. She also took the time to assess her skills to see what tasks she enjoyed doing most. Betsy realized she loved managing projects. Betsy created a career goal of finding work as a project manager at a company where she could be assigned to work in another country. She gave herself six months to try to find an American firm that would send her abroad, but also set a back up plan to save enough money so at the end of the six months, if she had no immediate job offers, she could quit her current job and take an extended overseas vacation to job hunt in person. I'm happy to report that Betsy found a job as a project manager after only two months and is overseas for the next year on assignment. I can't tell you how many times I have worked with clients whose Success Statement for career was not their own. Learning to seek out your own happiness, even at the risk of disappointing others, is a hard but important life lesson. Which would you rather do: Live a lifetime supporting other people's desires or a lifetime achieving your own? I'm sure you have heard phrases like, "you are responsible for your own happiness," or "the only person that can make you happy is you." Whatever the phrase, it's true. At the end of the day, it's up to you to find happiness and success with respect to career and any of the other key areas of life.

Success Statement Validation

To avoid making the same mistake as Betsy you need to recognize how key influencers in your life may be impacting your ability to write personally accurate Success Statements. Here's a short exercise that can help you:

Personal Perceptions Exercise

For each of the following people, write down five adjectives you would want them to use to describe you:

Mother
Father
Siblings
Spouse/Significant Other
Children
Extended Family (Grandparents, Aunts, Uncles, Cousins, etc.)
Friends
Co-workers
Managers
Strangers

Now, ask yourself two very important questions:

Question #1: For each of the people listed, did you choose five adjectives that you really want them to use to describe you, or did you write down five adjectives you feel they would want to be able to use to describe you? In other words, are the adjectives you selected based on what they want you to be to them, or what you have chosen to be to each of these people? (Hint: Did you use the same adjectives for each person? Of course you didn't, but why not?)

Can you see the difference? Often, we try to be what we believe others want us to be. What a difficult and useless goal. Many of the things one person would like us to be are in direct contrast to what another person wants. For example, is your *Career* Success Statement your own, or does it reflect what your parents or maybe your friends feel is the proper definition of career success? Keep in mind, there is no one "right" Success Statement; there is only one Success Statement that is right for you!

Question #2: Are your Success Statements your own, or are you trying to live up to someone else's definition of success?

In order to be successful, we need to stop trying to please others at the cost of sacrificing ourselves. Ask yourself if a desire to seek approval from any or all of the people above has ever caused you to compromise your goals. Moreover, ask yourself whether your definitions of success are your own, or if they represent the expectations of others. The sooner you clarify that your goals and definitions of success truly represent your own thoughts and feelings, the sooner you'll be able to achieve success.

In your notebook, take a moment to reflect and re-write your Success Statements if necessary. Make sure to eliminate any goals that don't serve your needs.

Ah-ha Moment: Are you living life on your own terms? Finding success in any area of life requires a strong understanding of your personal Success Statements. Unfortunately, many people never take the time to assess and develop statements that truly reflect their unique perspective on life. It's much easier to use the definitions of others (i.e. our parents, teachers, even society in general), as "default" definitions. However, this approach can create a lot of internal conflict. All too often, people go on to achieve success as defined by others, only to find this type of success unfulfilling. Ironically, the more success they achieve - the unhappier they become. Don't fall into the same trap. Do your soul searching now, find out what your true definitions for success are, and then stick to them! Don't let the opinions and expectations of others control your future. It is your life to live. At the end of the day, the only person you have to satisfy is yourself, so make sure you are working towards goals that support your happiness, not someone else's!

Personal Success Profile (a.k.a. PSP)

Now that you have prioritized your Core Values and have created Success Statements to help you determine the role you want career to play in your life, we can start identifying what the attributes of a "good" career are for you. This will require us to dig deeper in order to gain some perspective regarding your unique skills, abilities, passions and interests.

Why must you take the time to seek out and record this self knowledge? Because this kind of introspection helps to expand our viewpoints, increase our awareness and alter our perceptions. I'm not sure who said it, but there is a wonderful quote that says, "If we change the way we look at things, the things we look at change." By seeing something new in ourselves, we can change the way we see our world. Pretty profound, isn't it?

In this section, you will create a baseline state of understanding about yourself. In my coaching practice I refer to this as building a "Personal Success Profile" better known as a PSP. The PSP is simply a chart that summarizes your personal styles and preferences, as well as the action steps you can take to maximize your potential based on this self knowledge.

Ah-ha Moment: One of the biggest reasons for personal failure is the fact that many people never bother to try a new approach to their goal. It's more common for us to try repeatedly to achieve our goal by using the same method each time. There is an old saying, "If you do what you've always done, you'll get what you've always gotten." Are you guilty of not changing your approach? How many times have you tried to achieve your goal? Did you use the same method to achieve it each time? Could that be why you continue to fail?

A client of mine was always "on a diet," yet she never seemed to reach her weight loss goal. One day, I gently asked her if she knew why she was having so much trouble reaching her goal. She said, "Oh, it's my will power. I know what to do, it's just each time I start, I end up falling off the wagon." So I asked her when was the last time she actually made the effort to do some in depth assessment of herself to find which diet would work best with her. I also asked if she felt she was truly up-to-date on the latest research and findings with respect to diet. She admitted that she wasn't. I encouraged her to stop dieting and start learning. She agreed to give it a try. I'm happy to say my client made great strides. She not only identified some new approaches to diet, but she even took the time to research exercise in order to find a fitness routine she truly enjoyed. Seventeen pounds later and with a health report card from her doctor that in his own words was, "simply amazing," she was glowing with pride in her accomplishments.

Do you have a goal that you've never been able to achieve? Why not try looking for a new way to approach it? Just do your homework, and make sure it plays to your strengths. The reward for your efforts could be the ability to finally reach your elusive goal!

Creating Your PSP

So how do you create a PSP? In my coaching practice, I have clients complete tests and questionnaires which help them identify their personal styles and preferences in the following key areas:

- Interaction Style
- Learning Preferences
- Work Style
- Unique Gift
- Passions & Interests

Why are these areas important? Each represents a specific element of our character which shape and support our patterns of behavior, otherwise known as our habits. Breaking down this unique combination of personal traits also helps us understand how we interpret the world around us, and what impact they may be having on our ability to succeed. By taking the time to assess your styles and preferences in each of these areas, you will hopefully become aware of some important considerations when choosing a career path that supports your customized definition of career success.

Ah-ha Moment: As you complete each assessment, it will be up to you to analyze and interpret your results. While I have provided a fair amount of information to help you understand your styles and preferences, ultimately, it's your responsibility to take what you learn and use it to tailor your approach towards career. To make the most of these assessments, be sure to write down any revelations you have with respect to your unique traits and their impact on your ability to succeed. The more personal information you gather, the better your chances of identifying a career path that will provide long-term satisfaction.

It's time to start the self-discovery process! We'll begin by looking at one of the most important assessment elements: How you prefer to interact with the people and environment that surround you.

Interaction Style

An Interaction Style is the way in which we choose to communicate with others. It also reflects the way we interpret the actions of others. It even defines how we view and experience life.

Have you ever wondered why you get along with some people so much better than others? Have you ever noticed that some people know just what to say to get you angry? While you might be aware that this has to do with the different Interaction

Styles people possess, did you know your preferred style of interaction also affects your ability to succeed?

Each of us develops our Interaction Style based on how we perceive the world around us. We adjust or adapt our Interaction Style to help us cope with what we see, hear and feel. For example, in a room full of strangers, some people chose to be more outgoing, while others choose to be more reserved. Our Interaction Style is something we create over time. We use all of our experiences to develop an Interaction Style we feel can help us navigate life successfully. As a result, it is natural for us to feel most at ease with individuals who share the same Interaction Style or have an Interaction Style we respect.

However, did you ever stop to think that your Interaction Style also acts as a filter for information in your life? In other words, when you don't like or respect a particular Interaction Style, you're more apt to "tune out" or "ignore" what is being said. This means you could be missing out on valuable information that can help you achieve your goal. Conversely, if you actively seek out information that is presented to you in an Interaction Style you can relate to, you are able to learn and retain this information much quicker.

Moreover, your Interaction Style can also be a predictor of your behavior. To communicate in a certain manner requires us to act in a certain way. In fact, studies show that what we say represents only 7% of communication. The other 93% is the tone, facial expressions and body language we use to convey those words. If you've ever heard the phrase, "It's not what you say, but how you say it," then you know that each person's Interaction Style has a big impact on every interaction between themselves and others.

How people behave in certain situations provides great insight in to a person's Interaction Style. While each person has a unique personality, in my opinion, there are four general types of Interaction Styles that can be identified. While you may display some of the traits of each style from time-to-time, overall, each person has a particular style that is predominant. In short, everyone falls into one of these categories. They are:

Empathizer
Energizer
Contemplator
Commander

Before you determine your Interaction Style, let me stress that no one style is better than another. Each style has its own unique strengths. There are advantages to each of the Interaction Styles. In order to determine your style, complete the Interaction Inventory:

Interaction Style Assessment

For each of the questions in the following tables, circle the answer that is MOST like you. Tally the total number of circled answers in each column and record it in the space provided.

1.	Prefer to keep your opinions to yourself.	Prefer to state your views.
2.	Speak at a slower pace.	Speak at a faster pace.
3.	Minimal use of hand gestures.	Expressive via my hand gestures.
4.	Soft tone of voice.	Stronger tone of voice.
5.	More likely to ask questions.	Most likely to make comments.
6.	Do not like pressure situations.	Don't mind pressure situations if they can move things forward.
7.	Are careful to express yourself so not to offend others.	Are okay with expressing yourself even if others might not like it.
8.	Like to take enough time to resolve problems completely.	Prefer to move fast and resolve problems quickly.
9.	Are more relaxed in life.	Are more driven in life.
Total		
	A	**B**

1.	Are composed in discussions with others.	Are animated in discussions with others.
2.	More controlled body movement.	More expressive body movement.
3.	Use facial expressions infrequently.	Use facial expressions frequently.
4.	Appear reserved.	Appear outgoing.
5.	Act low-keyed.	Act with a sense of energy.
6.	Keep feelings private.	See sharing feelings with others as important.
7.	Prefer information and facts for making decisions.	Use feelings and instincts when making decisions.
8.	Feel logic works better than the heart.	Feel the heart is more important than logic.
9.	Like to jump right in and get going on work.	Utilize small talk and pleasantries before beginning work.
Total		
	C	**D**

Which of your scores is higher between A and B? ____
Which of your scores is higher between C and D? ____

If your two highest scores are:

A & C = Contemplator
B & C = Commander
A & D = Empathizer
B & D = Energizer

Now that you've determined your Interaction Style, let's take a look at it compared to the others. Take a moment to review the following chart to understand some of the basic characteristics of your preferred Interaction Style. Also take some time to review the other styles to see how they are both similar and different to your own.

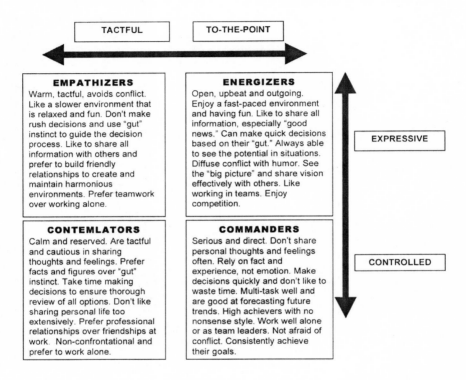

Can you see some advantages to each style? For example, Empathizers are seen as caring, while Commanders are viewed as focused. Energizers are often thought persuasive, while Contemplators are known to be calm. Every one of these Interaction Styles has strengths. But with strengths come weaknesses. For instance, how can someone be considered energetic if they are very calm? Let's take a look at how these same Interaction Styles can be disadvantageous.

When people are put in stressful situations, their Interaction Styles often display the weaknesses others see in them. Keep in mind, while you have chosen a certain Interaction Style for yourself, there are still three other Interaction Styles to consider. That means on average, 75% of the population does not choose to interact in the same way as you. So while you may feel the way you interact with others is highly effective, three out of four people could be misinterpreting your Interaction Style. The reality is your style has its perceived weaknesses by others. Keeping an open mind, take a look at the following descriptions of each Interaction Style to learn how some of the characteristics these styles display in more serious or stress-ful situations can be interpreted negatively by others. Be honest with yourself. Has use of your preferred Interaction Style ever resulted in you being seen as the fol-lowing?

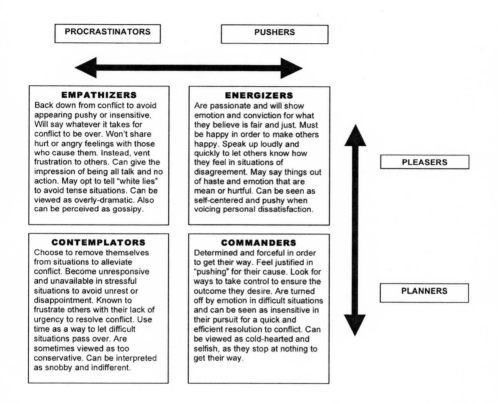

As you can see, there will be times when your style will work against you. While you may not intentionally try to give an impression of yourself as described above, from time-to-time, your Interaction Style will be the cause of some set backs in your efforts. It is your job to figure out what you can do to minimize the impact your preferred Interaction Style has on your ability to succeed.

In addition to assessing how your Interaction Style may be holding you back, you must also consider how the Interaction Style of others can hold you back from reaching your goals as well. Let me share an example:

Pete went to school and got his degree in physical therapy. He loved the work and hoped some day to manage a rehabilitation program, so he found a job in the reha-bilitation ward of a local hospital. Unfortunately, within a year, Pete was looking to change careers. When Pete and I sat down, we talked extensively about where and when his change in attitude toward his career goal came from. Pete shared the following: "Being the manager of a rehabilitation program isn't anything like I thought it would be. My manager is always overwhelmed with paperwork. She never has time to spend with the patients and doesn't feel she has the time or resources to put together programs for the patients that could really help in their therapy. She is out sick a lot and complains that the job is just too much to handle with a family. She has a lot of great ideas, and she shares them with us all the time, but she never gets the opportunity to implement them. Also, she promises a lot of things to the staff and then doesn't follow through. Don't get me wrong, she is a super nice, kind lady, but some people have gotten so frustrated with her that they've complained or quit. Yet nothing has changed. Just looking at her situation, I'd never want to be in her shoes."

After listening to Pete, I immediately had him complete the Interaction Style questionnaire. We determined that he was a Contemplator. However, at the same time, I had him profile his manager. He determined her to be an Empathizer. I then asked him to look at how his manager handled the job, given her Interaction Style, versus how he might handle the job with his Interaction Style. Pete answered, "Well, I probably wouldn't spend as much time as she does all day talking and chatting with people about their personal lives. She would probably have more time to get things done. I also wouldn't promise staff things just to make them smile. I would only commit to things I knew I could make happen." We went on to discuss the situation at length until Pete realized something very important: His manager's Interaction Style was impacting her ability to be successful at the job. Moreover, she was painting a picture of the job that was unattractive to Pete, yet Pete had never seen someone with a different style handle the job. His experience was limited. Pete realized that he needed to give his dream of becoming a manager of a rehabilitation program another shot. We focused on finding him a new job in physical therapy, but this time, Pete made sure that he selected a job where he felt the program director had an Interaction Style similar to his own. This would provide him with an opportunity to see if his own style worked well in this position. Pete ended up in a rehabilitation facility with a new manager who was a Commander. I spoke with Pete several months into his new job and he had this to say, "I'm very happy and recommitted to becoming a program manager. My new boss and I get along really well and he is helping me learn as much as I can. I may even be able to become assistant director here in the next few years. He handles the job extremely well. I'm so glad I found a place where the manager's Interaction Style was one I could respect and learn from. He is focused on the business like me, but he's more decisive than me. I also like that he is direct with staff. He's honest and only makes promises he can keep. He doesn't sugar-coat things and always tells us what we need to know. I've learned ten times more in the last three months because of this. It's had a huge impact on my career."

Pete was able to stay on track with his goal by recognizing the importance of having a manager whose Interaction Style works well with his own. Let's look at another example of how Interaction Style can hold you back from achieving your goals.

From the moment I met Carrie, I knew she was an Energizer. She was outgoing, creative and persuasive. She found the best in any situation and made everything fun and interesting. So imagine my surprise when Carrie came to me one day and secretly admitted she was very depressed about her job. Carrie was considered a top performer at her company and outwardly seemed to love her job, so I was puzzled. Carrie had this to say, "I feel unappreciated and underpaid. My work isn't exciting to me, yet I'm putting in so many hours each week, there is no time left for anything else in my life." Carrie and I went on to discuss what she had done so far to improve her situation. "Well, whenever I mention that I might be interested in finding a new job to one of my friends, they always tell me I'm crazy because I have it so good where I am. I've also tried to convey to my manager several times before that I would love to feel more challenged with my work, but all he ever does is offer me a new project to work on. Of course I end up taking the project, even if I don't want it, and then I'm just busier than I was before." Carrie was a classic example of someone who's Interaction Style was impacting her ability to succeed. As an Energizer, she prided herself on her ability to appear upbeat, positive and in control. Carrie's style makes her want to look successful to others, so she communicates to the world that she is happy with herself and her situation at all times. Having to admit that she was not pleased with her career was the ultimate failure to her. She would have rather hide her pain than show she wasn't happy with what she had. This element of her style was working against her goal to find a more satisfying career. I worked with Carrie to show her how her desire to look "perfect" in the eyes of others was holding her back. Moreover, I showed her how opening up to others and sharing her imperfections could help her overcome them. For example, sharing her desire to find more satisfaction in her career would generate conversations and support with friends and loved ones. It would also take the pressure off her to look and act like everything was fine. If she could get her dissatisfaction out in the open, she would be free to seek help and motivate herself towards her goal. At first, Carrie was hesitant about my comments. She wasn't thrilled that I was pointing to pride as her Interaction Style weakness. But after looking at the situation through my eyes, she had the following to say, "I guess I do tend to want to make my life look as attractive as possible. But it's because I feel like my life is good. Not to mention I really believe that life is what you make it. But you are right; I haven't been honest with myself or others about my feelings towards my career. Maybe opening up and showing my unhappiness can help me. I'm willing to give it a try." To help Carrie ease herself in to the approach of sharing her challenges with others, I encouraged her to set up some informational interviews with people she admired so she could review her current dilemma with them. Confiding in one or two people in a private setting instead of a large, open forum would help Carrie get used to sharing her true feelings with others.

After just one month, the change in Carrie was fantastic. "Letting people know how I feel about my career has been so helpful. I can't believe how many people have offered suggestions and help. I've learned a lot about other careers. I never realized how sharing concerns can help you to bond with others. Several of my friends said it was nice to see that I was actually "human." I had no idea how my Interaction Style was being perceived by the outside world. I was so surprised to learn that some people saw right through me and actually felt sorry for me because they knew I was working hard to make everything in my life look okay. I'm really reevaluating how I communicate. I know now that being overly positive and trying to make my world look perfect may not be the best thing."

As we can see from Carrie's example, our preferred Interaction Style will have its weaknesses. Yet if we can try to identify how those weaknesses could be impacting our ability to achieve our goals, we can take steps to work through them. As I said earlier, each Interaction Style has its strengths, but it's the weaknesses that we need to be even more aware of.

To make the self-assessment process easier, I have developed a chart which helps people use the characteristics of their preferred Interaction Style to identify which career elements would be most beneficial.

Can you see how your style impacts your ability to be happy in the job? Think of the one job in your past that you hated the most. Do you now have some insight as to why it wasn't a match for you?

In summary, Interaction Styles impact our ability to achieve goals in two ways.

First, the Interaction Styles of others have a direct impact on our perceptions of our career situation. You must make sure you recognize how people perceive things differently, based on their own Interaction Styles. Second, each Interaction

Style has its own set of strengths and weaknesses. Recognizing how they impact your ability to succeed can help to remove the roadblocks holding you back. The more you seek to understand all the Interaction Styles and the best way to make use of your unique strengths, the easier it will be to find ways to achieve your goals.

Let's continue to expand or self knowledge by taking a look at how you like to absorb new information. I'm referring to your Learning Preferences and how they impact your ability to be successful on-the-job.

If you are...	You will feel most comfortable with...				
	Work Environment	Co-workers	Management Style	Corporate Culture	Job Responsibilities
Empathizer	Comfortable, casual, organized.	Fun, friendly, kind, positive.	Warm, sympathetic, tactful, positive, but decisive to offset your emotion and tendency to procrastinate.	People first, profits second.	Customer support, employee relations, improvement projects.
Energizer	Attractive, comfortable, up-scale.	Fun, outgoing, competitive, positive, quick-minded.	Energetic, decisive, positive, supportive, but tactful to offset your passion and direct nature.	People and profits achieved simultaneously.	Sales, client/ employee training, roll-out of new company initiatives.
Contemplator	Well-organized, private, casual.	Respectful, pleasant, focused, fastidious independent.	Logical, articulate, honest, tactful, but decisive to offset your conservatism and tendency to wait to take action.	Profits with ethics.	Accounting, quality assurance, service evaluations.
Commander	Efficient, private, upscale.	Decisive, focused, quick-minded, competitive independent.	Logical, decisive, articulate, honest, but tactful to offset your seriousness and direct nature.	Profits are not personal.	Management, troubleshooting, reorganization, goal-setting.

Learning Preferences

It only makes sense that gaining perspective on yourself would include identifying the best ways for you to learn. I'm always surprised at the number of people who do not understand their unique combination of Learning Preferences. Have you ever wondered why some people can absorb more information from a book than others? Or why some folks can remember exactly what was said in a conversation? Understanding how you prefer to learn can help you identify careers that have the best learning environments for you. The more efficiently you learn, the stronger your ability to succeed in your chosen career.

Let's determine your Learning Preferences so you can identify what resources and methods for learning should be available to you in your next job.

Learning Preferences Assessment

For each of the questions listed, select your preferred answer from the columns to the right. Tally your answers at the end of each section.

Visual vs. Verbal

When reading a text book, I like to:	Go straight to the graphs, charts and pictures.	Read the text completely and ignore the graphs, charts and pictures.
In order to relax, I would rather:	Look at beautiful art, landscapes or other soothing pictorials.	Listen to music or a soothing voice.
If I had to learn something new quickly, I'd rather:	Observe someone doing what I need to learn or look at a picture book or video of the process.	Listen to a teacher or read a book describing what I need to learn.
What would you rather do?	Watch a movie with no sound.	Listen to a book on tape.
	Visual	**Verbal**

Active vs. Reflective

When learning something new I prefer to:	Get right in and try it out so I can learn from my mistakes.	Take time to think through how to execute what I've learned correctly, with minimal mistakes.
I like teachers who:	Give general instructions and then encourage us work on a problem on our own.	Give in-depth instruction and provide examples prior to having us try it out on our own.
I like to:	Work under pressure.	Have as much time as is needed to complete projects.
My general motto with regard to learning:	"Trial by error."	"Measure twice, cut once."
	Active	**Reflective**

Global vs. Sequential

To learn a new task, it's more important for me to know:	The ultimate purpose of the task and how it applies to my world.	The specific steps needed to be successful at the task, regardless of its purpose.
When it comes to learning a new theory, I prefer:	Understanding the "big picture" and thinking of the theory's possible applications in real life.	Learning as much detail as possible about executing the theory in real life.
When talking with someone casually, I prefer:	To talk about several different things in general.	Talk about one thing specifically and in great detail.
When presented with a new product, I like to think about:	How the product would work in my life?	The specific steps needed to use the product correctly.
	Global	**Sequential**

Now that you have identified your Learning Preferences in these three important areas, let's take a look at the strength and weakness of each preference.

Visual vs. Verbal

Visual learners prefer to see what they are learning. They prefer video to audio. Visual learners can watch someone complete a task and are able to repeat it quite easily.

Verbal learners prefer to hear what they are learning. They like to read a book or listen to presentations on a subject. Verbal learners can listen to someone describe something and repeat it back quite easily.

Visual learners do best in work environments in which you learn by observing. They can ask questions and see the answers, while Verbal learns do best in environments with lots of pre-instruction and discussion.

Active vs. Reflective

Active learners like the 'hands on' approach to learning. They prefer skipping the instructions and getting right to the learning through trial and error.

Reflective learners like to ask lots of questions and have plenty of time to absorb what they are learning. They prefer to review the process in their mind to ensure it is logical and consistent in order to avoid as much initial error as possible.

Active learners do best in work environments in which you learn by doing. On-the-job training is best for them. Reflective learners do best in work environments that provide extensive training programs and certification processes prior to beginning work in that area.

Global vs. Sequential

Global learners prefer to understand the 'big picture" with regard to what they are learning. They don't like to get bogged down in the details. They feel it is more important to understand the impact of what they are trying to achieve than the process they need to learn to achieve it. Global learners like instant gratification from their learning efforts.

Sequential learners feel it is more important to understand the proper steps for achievement than the implications of the achievement. Sequential learners like a logical, methodical process for learning. The more detail, the better. Sequential learners are patient learners.

Global learners do best in work environments that focus on getting results quickly. Shorter learning cycles, simpler objectives and the flexibility to adapt processes to meet their needs and interests are best for a Global learner. Sequential learners do best in work environments that are slower to achieve results. Less focus on the speed of achievement and a greater emphasis on quality, complexity and consistency are best for a Sequential learner.

Take A Personal Approach To Learning

Now that you've reviewed the characteristics of each style, can you see how important understanding your Learning Preferences is? Putting yourself in the wrong learning environment can hinder your success. Let me share an example with you.

By the time Jim came to me as a client, he had no confidence with regard to his career. "Every job I've had, I've failed at," he stated. Jim had graduated from college and, at the urging of his parents, had taken a job with a large financial planning company. Jim spent several months in training before he was assigned to a desk at a local branch of the company. Within two months he was on a performance evaluation. To avoid being fired, Jim found a new job at an insurance agency. Once again, he spent several months in training before returning to the agency. He was now coming to see me. He had been selling at the insurance agency for three months and it was pretty clear to Jim and his boss that it wasn't working. Jim was told he had two months to improve. "I just can't seem to get my act together," Jim told me. "My other friends seem to be really enjoying their jobs and are doing well. Why can't I?" I had Jim complete the Learning Preferences assessment. He profiled as Visual, Active and Global. Can you see what may have been the problem? Immediately, I began to share with Jim how his Learning Preferences were completely opposite of the styles of learning being used in his past and current job. Both the financial and insurance industries provide lots of verbal instruction. Jim preferred visual instruction. Additionally, both industries offer instruction over a long period of time so it can be reflected upon. Jim had learned lots of theories but no practical instruction was made available to him to support his Active learning style. Lastly, both financial and insurance industries require a lot of consistency with regards to their processes. There are complex, detail-oriented transactions required for success that must be completed in a precise, step-by-step process. This Sequential style did not support Jim's Global learning preference. Quickly, Jim realized he could be successful, if he could find a work environment where he could thrive. I continued working with Jim to identify careers that supported his unique Learning Preferences. I'm happy to say that Jim found work as a customer service representative for a software company. He was able to learn by observing other reps on live calls (Visual), he was taking calls after just three days of training (Active) and he was able to solve customer problems quickly using the knowledge he acquired as he went (Global). Jim was so much happier in his new role, he couldn't believe the difference. "This job was so easy to learn. It was fun and I found myself learning quickly. I feel really talented and productive here." Once Jim found a career that used his unique Learning Preferences, he was able to shine. "I was really worried that I was just a bad worker. Now I understand it wasn't me, it was the learning styles of my former employers that were holding me back." I'm pleased to say Jim is thriving in his new role and has already won an award for being a top performer.

In Jim's case, he had chosen careers that didn't use his unique Learning Preferences. Now consider when people chose the right career, but put themselves in the wrong learning environment. Here's an example:

Jen became certified as a personal trainer while in college. Upon graduating, she took a job back in her home town at a local gym. It was owned by an outgoing and successful man who had spent his career as a personal trainer before opening the gym. Jen was excited to be working for her new boss and was sure she would learn a great deal from him. By the time she came to me, she was convinced she had made the wrong choice of careers and after only six months working at the gym, was considering leaving the fitness industry all together. I asked Jen to describe why she felt she had made the wrong choice. Jen said, "Well, I thought being a personal trainer would be fun. I would create customized exercise and diet plans for my clients and I would work with them over several months to help them achieve their goals of making health and wellness a priority in their lives. But after six months, I feel like I don't have the ability to make people stick with their goals and make the changes they need to succeed." I asked Jen to give me an example. "Well, when new clients come to the gym, I'm responsible for giving them a tour and sharing with them our philosophy for helping them reach their goals. But it seems like each time I introduce the client to the owner, he is able to answer their questions so much better than me that he has to take over. After that, the client only wants to work with him. I just don't think I have the skills to build a clientele base. No one seems to want to work with me." At this point I asked Jen what kind of training she had received from the owner. She responded, "Nothing formal. He just suggested that I follow him around and listen to how he handles clients. He believes in on-the-job training." I asked how Jen felt that was working. She admitted that she had found it difficult. "He has a very different personality than me. I just don't see myself saying a lot of the things he says to clients. So I find it hard to put what he says into my own words." I then asked Jen to describe what her boss suggested she do at the gym to help her get familiar with building customized fitness programs. She said he encouraged her to jump in and introduce herself to the club members, offering them free advice and help on their workouts. When I asked how that was going Jen said, "Not too well. I just don't feel comfortable interrupting people and offering up advice without first getting to know them and their needs. I was trained at school to do a full assessment of a person's health and fitness level before offering suggestions, so I'm nervous about making recommendations without first having all the facts." Lastly, I asked Jen to tell me how her boss was assessing her performance on the job. She said, "I know he is not happy with me. He keeps telling me that I should be 'bringing in more business' and raising the 'headcount' to the gym, but I don't see how that meets the goal of helping people improve their health and fitness. It just has them spend money on a membership; it doesn't help them reach their personal goals."

It was clear that while Jen was in the right career, she was in the wrong place. I had Jen take the Learning Preferences assessment. Her results were Visual, Reflective and Sequential. Can you see her problem? Jen's boss offered a work environment that did not support Jen's Learning Preferences. He was a Verbal instructor who expected Jen to know how to implement what he was stating without first showing her. Second, he expected Jen to learn by actively working with clients. Jen's experience and training made it hard for her to ethically "jump in" and help people. She preferred following the proven process she had been given to assess a client's needs, which included a fair amount of thought and reflection before making recommendations. Last, her boss was looking for the short-term gains of membership sales and expected Jen to figure out what she needed to do in the job to make that happen. Jen wanted to be able to take her time and see the success of her clients as the long-term goal she should be achieving. I spent time with Jen, showing her these differences. Jen was able to see that she needed to find a job as a personal trainer that offered the ability to use the Learning Preferences she was most comfortable with. With this as her focus, Jen sought and found a job at a rehabilitation center. The center was part of a large hospital network. There, Jen received extensive training and even got some additional certification before she was allowed to work with clients. Jen was given a well-defined process to follow when working with patients that was consistently enforced throughout the facility. But best of all, Jen's performance was based on her ability to see measurable improvements in her client's health. Jen learned how to improve her skills to meet these needs. "I can't believe I almost gave up a career I love, just because I wasn't in the right learning environment for me." When I followed up with her a month later, Jen reported: "I love my work and have learned more in one month here than my entire time at the gym."

Recognizing how you prefer to learn and what you should look for in a learning environment to support you preferences can have a profound impact on how quickly you find success in your career. Review your Learning Preferences and take note of the characteristics that will create your ideal learning environment.

You are now armed with the knowledge of how to maximize your Learning Preferences. It's time to move on and determine your Work Style.

If you are...	You will thrive in a work environment with this kind of....		
	Training	Support Tools	Performance Criterion
Visual	Observe, watch videos or 'live' instruction.	Computers, pictures, graphs and the ability to watch and learn from others doing the same job.	You can watch how to do something and be able to repeat it.
Verbal	Listen, read books or attend presentations.	Telephones, books, audio cassettes, computers and the opportunity to listen to others doing the same job.	You can listen how to do something and repeat it.
Active	Hands-on. Live role-playing.	Learn on-the-job. Be independent and complete tasks through trial-and-error.	You can jump into a situation quickly and be helpful as you learn, confident that you can fix your mistakes and learn from them as you go.
Reflective	Hands-off, analysis and hypothesis review.	Contemplate and strategize before attempting a solution. Research and make informed decisions.	You can refrain from diving in until you are certain you can be highly effective when you start working.
Global	Key points only as they relate to achieving the short-term goal.	Understand the short-term goal and identify basics you need to know to get started.	You can work at a faster pace, utilize creativity and use short-cuts when necessary to get the quickest ROI.
Sequential	Extensive steps and logical progression to long-term objective.	Understand the long-term goal and identify and complete ever step necessary to complete the job from start to finish consistently.	You can work at a slower-pace, exercise restraint, follow detailed instructions and be thorough in completing processes to ensure the greatest ROI.

Work Style

Any goal worth achieving will require some degree of effort. This effort will be broken down into manageable steps and executed with care. Understanding how you like to complete tasks can have a significant effect on how you approach your goal. This is referred to as your Work Style.

There are four general ways in which people prefer to work. While individuals may choose to use all of the Work Style types at different times, there is usually one style that is predominantly used to complete the majority of their tasks.

This is especially true in your career. Let's look at the obvious: A job involves you working. So doesn't it make sense that in order to maximize your productivity on the job, you should find a career that lets you work predominately in your preferred Work Style? Let's determine your primary Work Style by completing the following test.

Work Style Assessment

For each of the questions in the first column, circle the best answer for you from the four choices listed to the right of the question. Once completed tally your scores to see which Work Style you prefer.

To Identify Your Work Style: Tally the total number of answers you circled in each column and record it in the space provided. The column with the highest score is your preferred Work Style.

Now that you've identified your preferred Work Style, you can use it to help you determine the right career for you. For example, most successful personal assistants and office support staff are strong Administrators, while Architects make great product designers and marketing executives. If you are a Reporter, you may want to consider a career in sales, customer service or training. If you're a Facilitator, you should consider being a project manager or entrepreneur.

Your career success will be dependent upon your ability to use your preferred Work Style as much as possible. Why? Because you are most energized and feel most productive and satisfied when you are using your preferred style. Take a look at the definitions of each style below. Can you see the advantages of each one?

Your company is having a brainstorming session and each employee gets to pick which problem they want to work on, which would you pick?	Come up with some new ideas for products and/or services your company could sell to grow the business.	Come up with some new processes to streamline work at the office in order to save time and money.	Develop the marketing message and training materials to support a new company initiative.	Prioritize the company's biggest challenges in the coming year and identify some action steps to be taken by each department to help solve these challenges.
Which phrase best describes your most valued attributes on-the-job?	Creative and innovative.	Well-organized and efficient.	Well-connected and in-the-know.	Highly-productive and good with unexpected changes.
Which of the following tasks would you find most fun to do?	Come up with a new design for a file cabinet.	Set-up and complete the filing for the new cabinet.	Present the features and benefits of the new file cabinet design.	Set up a plan for selling the new file cabinet design.
If someone asked you to create a "to do" list, which one best describes what you would write down?	A list of all the things I would love to try in my lifetime.	A list of every task, in detail, I need to complete today.	A list of all the people I need to speak to and/or meet with in the next week and what they will be helping me with.	A list of goals I intend to complete in the next 3-6 months.
When you first arrive at work, what do you like to do?	Start thinking about the most interesting way for you to tackle a new project.	Organize your desk and take care of any daily tasks that need to be completed.	Say 'hello' to all of your coworkers and get caught up on the latest company news.	Review your goal list and prioritize your day for maximum ROI of your time.
Total				
	ARCHITECT	**ADMINISTRATOR**	**REPORTER**	**FACILITATOR**

ARCHITECT	ADMINISTRATOR	REPORTER	FACILITATOR
• Likes to brainstorm ideas. • Enjoys planning projects. • Prefers to think in "big picture" as opposed to being bogged down with excessive details. • Enjoys developing new ways to accomplish tasks and improve performance.	• Loves to organize information and tasks. • Creates systems for keeping things running smoothly. • Prefers to have everything "in order" before beginning work on a project. • Doesn't like changes or disruptions to the processes and procedures they have created.	• Likes to share and seek out information. • Enjoys working with all types of people to build strong relationships and learn more about various business situations. • Prefers face-to-face meetings and live calls to voicemail and e-mail.	• Enjoys creating "to do" lists so they can check off their accomplishments. • Doesn't like to waste time at work. • Prefers a structured yet flexible schedule. • Prefers working on tasks that will provide the greatest ROI for their personal goals.

How can the inability to use your Work Style hinder your career success? Let's take a look.

When Jerry came to me, she was looking to make a career change because she felt she had missed her "calling in life." Jerry was currently employed as human resources representative for a large software firm. She was responsible for hiring all company employees. She also was responsible for counseling employees who weren't performing and when necessary, letting them go. While the pay was good, and the job was interesting, Jerry still felt that she wasn't in the right career for her. She was looking to be more fulfilled in her work. I had Jerry complete my standard PSP tests, including the Work Style assessment. When I saw that Jerry was an Administrator, I knew her problem immediately. I began by asking Jerry about her favorite part of her day on the job. Jerry said, "That's easy, I like the morning and the evening because I get a chance to complete my paperwork in peace and get my desk cleaned up and organized." I asked what she liked least about her work. She said, "I find talking to all of the employees stressful. Everyone has issues they want to discuss. I also find the interviewing of the new employees boring. They all say the same thing." It was clear that while Jerry was an Administrator, the majority of her job required her to be a Reporter. Speaking and working with people all day was not energizing Jerry; it was draining her. So I asked Jerry the following, "What if you could find a job that let you spend the day organizing things?" While Jerry agreed that this would be more exciting to her, she didn't see how she could just leave her job to find one that allowed her to specialize in organization. I then asked, "What if you could have a job with your current employer that allowed you to do more of what you love?" Jerry agreed that this would be an attractive option, but that there was no such job in her company. To which I replied, "Why not create one?" Jerry looked at me in disbelief, but once I described my proposal to her it all made sense. A long-term employee of the company with an Administrator Work Style, Jerry was acutely aware of all the things she knew could be better organized and managed at her company. I had her build a new job description which described what she could do, using her Administrator Work Style to help her company. I encouraged Jerry to present the job concept to her manager with the promise of training the person who would replace her as a recruiting specialist. To Jerry's surprise, the company was thrilled with the proposal. Her initiative paid off. They were happy to see these problems taken over by a knowledgeable employee. They didn't want to lose Jerry, so by giving her a new job she enjoyed, they were able to keep her knowledge at the company and use her expertise in another way. Jerry was thrilled with the change. "I'm much happier in my new role. I help each of the department managers get more organized with their corporate paperwork and help each one develop a personalized process to stay on top of it. I even helped select my replacement and made sure that she preferred the Reporter Work Style. She is doing a great job and I couldn't be happier."

So often, clients like the company they work for, but the job they are doing doesn't make the best use of their Work Style. The good news is that if you are a valued employee of the company, you may have the opportunity to do what Jerry did. Identifying and creating a job description that uses your Work Style to its fullest is a great way for you to find greater career satisfaction, and offers your company the opportunity to get even more productivity from you. It's a win-win situation!

But what do you do if your company doesn't have the ability to let you reinvent your job? Let's take a look:

Mike was selling business software when he came to me. He had joined the company a year earlier because in his own words, "I thought the software was really innovative and I could see how it could be used in so many different ways by customers. I was sure it would practically sell itself." Unfortunately, that was not the case. While Mike knew how the software worked inside and out, he just wasn't making his quota. In fact, he hated selling altogether and had come to me in hopes of finding a new career direction. When Mike completed the PSP tests, I saw that his problem was related to his Work Style preference. Mike was an Architect but his job required him to be a Reporter. While Mike was good at brainstorming and determining all the different ways in which his company's software could be used effectively by clients, Mike wasn't comfortable convincing clients of all the reasons why they needed to buy the software. "I just don't like stating the obvious to the client. I feel like I'm pushing the software on them. It would be so much easier if they would tell me what they wanted the software to do and I could tell them how to customize it. Instead, I have to sell them on all the features of the software, and I'm just not good at that." It was clear Mike would be better off in a technical support role, helping clients who had already bought the software, showing them how to use it to its fullest potential. Here's the catch. Mike's company didn't offer support for their software. They outsourced their support to a company located in another state. So the opportunity to switch jobs within the company was not an option. Mike and I worked together until he realized he needed to find another job. But armed with his new found PSP knowledge, in particular, his preferred Work Style as an Architect, Mike focused on finding jobs that would allow him to be creative and design solutions without the requirement to sell. Mike eventually found a job as a solutions specialist with another software firm. In this job, Mike got to partner with a sales rep. The rep was responsible for selling the product, while Mike was responsible for working with the client to show them exactly how the software needed to integrate into their business for maximum ROI. "I love my new job." Mike said. "I get to do what I love and help sell the product, without all the pressure of being solely responsible for the sale."

As you can see, finding a career that supports your Work Style can make all the difference with regard to your career satisfaction and success. Now that you've determined your preferred Work Style, let's review some key things to keep in mind when choosing a career.

You are almost done with the PSP assessment process. Soon you will have all the information needed to take a more customized and effective approach to reaching your career goals. So let's continue by recognizing what you have to offer the "working world."

If you are an...	You will work best in this....		
	Positions Involving	Performance Criterion	Pressure Level
Architect	Creativity, customized solutions and problem solving.	Your ability to look at each situation and think-outside-the-box to identify the ideal solution.	Low: Creativity shouldn't be rushed.
Administrator	Organization, consolidation and streamlining.	Your ability to look at each situation and find the commonality that can be used to make it more organized and consistent.	Moderate: Deadlines are okay, but only when there is plenty of advanced notice for planning proper execution and timely completion.
Reporter	Sharing, motivating and persuading.	Your ability to articulate information in a way that gets others to act.	Moderate: Time-sensitive goals are okay, but only when you are given all the information you need to be able to articulate and persuade your audience in an effective and timely fashion. You don't want to appear desperate.
Facilitator	Prioritizing, decision-making, and troubleshooting.	Your ability to recognize what needs to be done and take action quickly in order to seize upon opportunities and minimize unexpected problems.	High: You work well under pressure and enjoy competing against the clock. It helps you to crystallize what's most important and gets you moving.

What Is Your Unique Gift?

We must not give only what we have; we must give what we are.—Cardinal Mercia

When I ask clients to share with me what they feel their Unique Gift is, I usually get either a blank stare or a little chuckle. Most people don't really take the time to consider what their gift is. Some people think the idea of identifying one's Unique Gift is silly or self-absorbed. I would argue that identifying and using your Unique Gift, especially in your career, is one of the smartest and most unselfish things you can do. As an adult, we have a lifetime of experiences that have helped us determine what we are good at. Every day, we experience things that we unconsciously assess. Your subconscious regularly assesses and evaluates your performance on every task you complete or fail to complete throughout the day. Even the littlest tasks are assessed: "Did I brush my teeth well this morning, or did I rush? Did I drive safely to work, or did I drive recklessly to get there on time?" We evaluate ourselves so much that it may be hard to imagine we are good at anything. But the truth is this ability to evaluate ourselves has also given us the opportunity to identify those things we are good at. Over the years, everyone excels at certain things. As a result, without even knowing it, you have fine-tuned your skills for this gift out of your recognition of your ability to do it well. How? Well, when we are good at something we tend to be more interested in it. The more we learn the better we become. Additionally, when we excel at something we tend to seek out more opportunities to do it. Practice makes perfect. The simple fact is: Doing something well makes us feel satisfied and happy. Everyone has a Unique Gift; a special skill, a natural ability. By identifying it, you can be even more proactive at using it. Using your gift is the best way to help yourself and others. It brings out the best in you, and it enables you to give something back. Your Unique Gift can be identified by asking yourself these simple questions:

1. What do my friends and family regularly ask for my advice or help on?
2. What skill do I continually find interesting and seek more knowledge to perfect?
3. What skill do I use on a regular basis that gives me a sense of satisfaction and happiness when I use it?

Don't be humble; it's time to determine your Unique Gift. Take a moment to write it down in your notebook.

My Unique Gift is:

Are you still having trouble determining your Unique Gift? Then try this:

Answer the following questions in as much detail as you can. If you are struggling to find the answers, feel free to consult friends and family to give you additional perspective.

1. Describe the one accomplishment you are most proud of. What challenges did you overcome, what did you learn from the experience, and how do you use what you've learned to help yourself and others?

2. Describe the most memorable thing you've done to help another person. What was it, why did you choose to do it, how do you know it helped?

3. What was the last thing a family member asked you for advice on? Did they take your advice? Do they ask for your advice often?

4. What was the last thing a friend asked you for advice on? Did they take your advice? Do they ask for your advice often?

5. Imagine you have passed away and are in spirit at your eulogy. What would your friends and family say about you? How would they describe you? What traits would they be most complimentary of? What would they say they would miss most about you?

Were you able to see some patterns in your answers? What do you seem to do well? Are you afraid that your Unique Gift isn't worthy? Do you feel like the one thing you do well isn't important or significant? Whatever your Unique Gift is, I guarantee it is important and worthy of incorporating into your career. Let me show you:

I had a client, Sarah, come to me because she felt she was incapable of ever finding a career. "I don't want a job with 9 to 5 hours, I hate offices and computers, and I don't like getting dressed up." Sarah couldn't find a job that sounded appealing. Her parents were pushing hard for her to at least find something she could make some money at. But Sarah refused to take a job she hated just for a paycheck. "It's against my principals," she told me. "I want to find work that doesn't feel like work, you know?" I understood what Sarah meant and had her complete the PSP assessment tests, but it wasn't until she identified her Unique Gift that a real Ah-ha Moment occurred. At first, Sarah bluntly told me she had no Unique Gift. "That's my problem. I'm not good at anything people do for work." But the more we talked, the more Sarah opened up. Finally, she said, "Well, I am good at creating atmosphere, but that's not a Unique Gift." I seized the opportunity and asked what she meant by 'atmosphere.' Sarah replied, "I love helping people design spaces that set a mood, you know, 'atmosphere.' For example, I'm happiest when I'm helping my friends and family decorate or organize a room. I love helping people create a space that reflects their personality and style." I asked her to give me some examples, "Well, all of my friends ask me to help them go shopping for new furniture and accessories because they say I have a great eye for what they would like. But what good does that do me?" I followed up her question with my own, "Would you say you are talented when it comes to decorating?"

Sarah said, "Yes, I guess so, but I don't feel being an interior designer is important. I want a job that does something truly valuable, something respectable," she responded. So I went on and asked, "Are these rooms you help people decorate important to them?" Sarah said, "Of course, that's why they want them to be special. It's where they live their lives. They want to feel comfortable and inspired. They want a space that makes them feel good about themselves." That's when it hit her. She did have a Unique Gift and it was important. "I get it." Sarah said. "What I do is valuable to others. Even though it's easy for me to create a beautiful space, for them, the idea of decorating their home is quite stressful. What you're saying is that people respect my ability to design." Sarah finally saw that her Unique Gift was anything but frivolous or unimportant. Making other people happy is a special and significant gift. Now it was time for her to use it. Sarah found a job as an assistant to a busy interior designer. Sarah was an instant hit and in no time was working side-by-side with the designer. Sarah went back to night school and got her degree in interior design. She eventually built up her reputation and went out on her own. In her own words, "Who would have thought that the girl who hated work would someday be her own boss!"

Don't discount or ignore your Unique Gift. No matter what it is, it needs to be used. The people with the greatest level of career satisfaction are the ones who have found a way to use their Unique Gift on a daily basis. It's time to consider how you are going to use yours!

Passions & Interests

Pleasure in the job puts perfection in the work.—Aristotle

In addition to your Unique Gift, you will also want to become acutely aware of your Passions & Interests. Why? Because our Passions & Interests give us good examples of how we have been able to utilize our personal styles and preferences effectively together. In short, when we enjoy something, it's because we are collectively using our styles and preferences to their fullest. Moreover, analyzing our Passions & Interests can help us anticipate how we might like something we've never tried before. For example, wouldn't it be nice to know in advance if a particular career might be a good fit for us? If we can compare the career to some of our Passions & Interests to assess its potential for satisfying us, we can improve the chances of finding and choosing the best career options.

Over the years, I've developed a standard set of questions I have clients answer to help them analyze their Passions & Interests. Take a moment now to answer each of these questions in as much detail as possible. Record your answers in your notebook.

1. List all the sports and hobbies you like to play, do, and/or watch.

2. What are the most common types of T.V. shows that you stop to watch when channel surfing?

3. Are there any particular shows or events that you try hard not to miss? If so, why do you like them?

4. What kinds of "live" events would you pay money to go see?

5. List at least three people you admire and why?

6. If you could visit five places, anywhere in the world, where would they be and why?

7. If you could have free training to become an expert at anything you wanted, pick three things you would get trained to do?

8. When you go shopping in a mall, what stores do you typically browse in?

9. What magazines do you read regularly?

10. What kinds of books do you like to read? What subjects interest you the most?

11. If you were given a million dollars and told to spend it in one week, what kinds of things would you buy?

12. If you were given all the time and resources you needed to relax and do anything you wanted, how would you fill your time?

Analyze Your Responses

Now it's time for you to review your answers. What are you looking for? The goal is to be able identify how your styles and preferences influence your behavior. By using what you've learned about yourself so far, you can start to see patterns and themes in your answers that illustrate your unique styles and preferences. Once you see who you are, you'll have an easier time identifying what kind of career would make you the happiest. In fact, you will be able to be much more proactive towards every key area of your life!

Take a look at the following table. Each section has a series of questions you can ask yourself about your Passions & Interests that relate to the various styles and preferences you've assessed about yourself so far. Take a moment to reflect and record your answers in the space provided.

Core Values	
How are your Core Values reflected in your Passions & Interests?	
How do the hobbies and sports you participate in, your T.V., magazine, book choices, and your desired travel destinations support your priorities?	
Does the way in which you would spend $1 million or spend your time relaxing support your priorities?	
Why have you never pursued being trained in the things you are interested in? What would you have to sacrifice to be trained? What areas of your life now are not worth giving up for the chance to pursue your dream?	
How similar are the Core Values of the people you admire to your own? Are they the same, or do you admire them because their priorities are different from your own? What does that say about your Core Value ranking?	
Interaction Style	
What are the themes of the shows you watch on T.V. and the magazines and books you read? Are they self-help oriented? Are they competitive? Are they focused on helping others? Are they about creating beauty and serenity? Are they factual and historical? How do these shows support your Interaction Style?	
What do you admire about the people you listed? Is their style similar to your own, or do you admire a quality they possess that you don't?	
How is your Interaction Style reflected in your dream travel destinations, the way in which you would spend $1 million, and even the way in which you would relax and spend unlimited free time?	
Do you know how to enjoy yourself with limited resources or do you rely on people, places, and/or specific resources to make you happy?	

Learning Preferences	
How are the things you like to watch on T.V. or read in books and magazines reflective of your Learning Preferences? Does their subject matter or method in presenting information work well with your preferences?	
How are your Learning Preferences reflected in the hobbies and sports you participate in?	
What kind of training do the careers you chose require? Would you enjoy that training? Why?	
Work Style	
How does your choice of hobbies make use of your preferred Work Style?	
Do you tend to like team sports and hobbies or do you prefer sports and hobbies you do individually? Why is that? Are you more comfortable working with others or alone?	
Are the places you wish to visit serene or busy, fast-paced or relaxed, full of people or void of people, old or new, big or small, etc?	
How do the people you admire work? Are they successful because of their Work Style? If so, is it similar or different from your own? What does your admiration for them say about your own preferences?	
Unique Gift	
Which of your Passions & Interests requires you to use your Unique Gift? How do you fine-tune your gift?	
How might you use your Unique Gift with your Passions & Interests to create a career you found satisfying?	
What are the Unique Gifts of the people you admire? Are they similar to your own? If not, why do you think you admire their gifts? Would they admire yours?	

These are just a few of the questions you can ask yourself. It's time to do some soul searching. The goal is to have some Ah-ha Moments with respect to your patterns of behavior. Why do you like what you like? Where did your Passions & Interests originate? Learn as much as you can about your Passions & Interests and you'll find it easier to identify careers that incorporate what you care about. Remember Sarah? She wanted to find work that didn't feel like work. Don't we all? Finding a career that keeps you as motivated and happy as your Passions & Interests do is the best way to make work fun! Let me share with you an example.

A client, Jeff, came to me because he wanted to get out of his career as a sporting event coordinator. His job was very exciting and prestigious, as he worked with many high-profile sports stars. Jeff loved his work, but he was recently married and had a new baby boy. The idea of relocating his family every year to the event's new location was not something he wanted to do. Moreover, now that they were a family, Jeff and his wife wanted to be closer to their own extended families as well. Unfortunately, Jeff was having a very hard time finding another career that interested him. "I can't envision doing anything else," he commented. "I love sports. I live for sports. I can't imagine doing something not related to sports," Jeff said. Moreover, Jeff's income level was going to be hard to maintain if he switched careers. He was going to have to start over in a new career and work his way up again. Jeff was really frustrated. "I feel like I've created a dead end for myself. I want to earn a good living for my family, but I can't find anything that would make me as happy. I just don't want to take a job I'll be miserable in." To make things more complicated, Jeff eventually quit his sporting event position because he did not want to relocate his family again. So the pressure was on for Jeff to find work. I had Jeff complete the PSP assessment tests to learn more about himself. Here is a summary of Jeff's PSP:

Core Value Ranking	Significant Other Family & Friends, Mental Self Physical Self Career Fun & Recreation Finances Physical Surroundings
Interaction Style	Energizer
Learning Preferences	Verbal, Active, Global
Work Style	Facilitator
Unique Gift	Solving Time-Sensitive Problems Quickly, a.k.a. Putting Out Fires

While the results of the PSP tests were enlightening, it wasn't until we finally reviewed Jeff's Passions & Interests that it all came together so that he could finally see some career transition possibilities. Jeff was definitely crazy about sports; his list was a mile long. But he was also interested in other things. He loved music and attending shows. It was clear he enjoyed experiencing life. "Good food, good friends, and good times," could have been Jeff's motto. What ever he did, he liked to do it to the hilt, revealing a clear pattern. Jeff was interested in all things that allowed him to interact with people. Moreover, he enjoyed stimulating activities that were exciting and fun. Jeff's Passions & Interests were fast-paced and energetic. He preferred variety.

I asked Jeff the following question, "Besides your love of sports, what parts of your job as a sport event coordinator supports your Passions & Interests?" Jeff contemplated the question for a while and said, "I think my ability to attend events and be involved in the experience is good for me. I really enjoy participating in the events because it helps me identify what I can do to make them better the following year. I also have a chance to fix any unexpected problems myself." I asked him to dig deeper. "Well, I guess I enjoy all the interaction with people. The celebrities, the executive sponsors and even the attendees. I love talking with them and getting feedback about the event," Jeff stated. He went on, "I also love the excitement and energy at an event. There's so much anticipation leading up to the big day, and then the day comes and goes in a flash. I always look forward to getting to the event early because my day is so unexpected. I have so many things to juggle at once, I enjoy multi-tasking." I had Jeff look at his assessment results and compare them to what he had just described to me. It suddenly became clear to Jeff why he had wanted to find a career that allowed him to continue to experience all of these things. His job as an event coordinator had used so many of his styles and preferences effectively, he'd be crazy not to find a new job that used them as well, if not better. The key was to find a job as an event coordinator that didn't require him to move. So I had Jeff brainstorm by asking him the following: "Where could you work which would allow you to stay in one place and coordinate large events that would enable you to experience the event, network with the attendees and feel the energy and excitement created from the event? In other words, where do these events occur?" The question seemed to turn a light bulb on in Jeff's head. He burst out, "At stadiums!" Jeff realized he could continue doing what he loved for an arena. "They host sporting, music and all sorts of other events - even children's shows." Jeff used his contacts to start researching and setting up informational interviews with stadium executives. While the competition was tough for these popular and rare jobs, Jeff had a strong resumé. He was patient and soon found work at a new, mid-sized arena built for a local university. His job was to identify the appropriate sized events for the arena. He was involved in all aspects of the arena business and couldn't be happier. "I knew I was in the right job for me, I just needed to look at my Passions & Interests to see that I wasn't just interested in sports, but rather the work experience sporting events offered."

Analyzing your Passions & Interests to see how they've been shaped by your styles and preferences is invaluable. We must look beyond the interests we are passionate about and determine why we are drawn to them. It can unlock valuable self knowledge that can power our way to true career satisfaction.

Knowledge Is Power

When love and skill work together, expect a masterpiece.—John Ruskin

Now that you understand the "Gain Perspective" element to personal success, the phrase, "knowledge is power" has a whole new meaning. The knowledge you've acquired about yourself is going to help remove the roadblocks which have hampered your past efforts. You now have the ability to identify action steps that can help you make the most of your unique combination of styles and preferences. Below is a PSP Summary Sheet. Take a moment now to create this form in your notebook and record the results of the PSP assessment tools you've just completed. Next, review and summarize all of your strengths for each element listed. Last, using this detailed self knowledge, identify what you will want to consider when looking for a career path with respect to each one.

PSP Summary Sheet

	Assessment Results	My Strengths	How will I use this
information to identify a career path that's right for me?			
Core Value Ranking			
Interaction Style			
Learning Preferences			
Work Style			
Unique Gift			
Passions & Interests			

Once you have completed the PSP Summary Sheet, find a way to mark that page for quick reference. We'll be referring back to it soon; however, it's time to move on. You've completed the first step of **The G.L.O.W. Method** and are now ready for the next step: Identifying and setting an effective career goal.

PART II

THE G.L.O.W. METHOD: Luminate Your Goal

STEP 2: Luminate Your Goal

When I stand before God at the end of my life, I would hope that I would not have a single bit of talent left and I could say, "I used everything that you gave me." — Erma Bombeck

Now that you've taken the time and energy to develop a PSP, you are finally ready to create a detailed career goal. "Luminate Your Goal" is the step in which you use what you've learned thus far to develop a career goal you are 100% certain is achievable. You will use customized tools to qualify and quantify your goal, which will also serve to build your confidence in your ability to achieve it. In essence, you are going to "light up" your career objectives, by taking the proper steps to ensure they work with your unique styles and preferences. You'll begin by developing a list of career criteria.

Creating A Career Criteria List

With your values, styles and preferences well-defined, it's time to find a career path you can embrace. To begin, you must create a Career Criteria List that supports your Success Statement. A Career Criteria List is a very specific outline of what your ideal job should be. It lists, in as much detail as possible, all the characteristics you believe your next career will require in order for you to achieve career success as you've defined it. Follow the exercise below to create a comprehensive Career Criterion List.

Must-haves, Nice-to-haves & Don't-wants

To make an effective list you must begin by identifying all of your perceived needs and wants, as well as all of the things you don't want. What's the difference? Look at the following definitions:

Must-haves: These are your needs, a characteristic of the career that must be present in order for you to accept it. (i.e. the minimum amount of salary you can afford to live on.)

Nice-to-haves: These are your wants. While wants are not necessities, they make the career more attractive. Because wants potentially enhance your career satisfaction, (3-weeks vacation instead of the standard 2-weeks per year, e.g.), wants can significantly impact your career decision when present.

Don't-wants: These are things that would make the career less attractive, such as required overtime that might result in the need to stay late or work weekends. You would still consider accepting a job when Don't-wants exist, but the reduction in career satisfaction they might cause affects your decision.

STEP 1: In your notebook, create a table like the one shown here and then take a moment to write down your Must-haves, Nice-to-haves and Don't-wants for each of the career criteria listed. Under "miscellaneous" be sure to add any additional items not already identified that are important to your career satisfaction.

	Must-have	Nice-to-have	Don't-want
Salary			
Benefits			
Corporate Culture			
Management Style			
Location			
Styles & Preferences to be Leveraged			
Skills & Abilities to be Used			
Performance Evaluation Criteria			
Co-workers			
Work Environment			
Training & Support Resource			
Hours/Days Worked			
Opportunity for Growth			
Other			

Ah-ha Moment: If you are just starting out in the workforce, you may find your Career Criteria List to be quite small. That's good! The less you require of your career in order for you to be satisfied the better. Over time, people often place more and more requirements on their career, making it even more difficult to find career satisfaction. As you create your list, be sure to only put down the most important elements for your happiness. And if you're a workforce warrior with a long list of criteria, I encourage you to go back and really reassess what's important to you. What can you do to trim the list down? Be honest with yourself and accept that your career cannot and should not solve all of life's challenges. Instead, see what other areas of your life you could change so that your career doesn't have to carry the weight of your happiness.

For example: Look at the salary amount you listed. What lifestyle does that support? Does it really need to be that high, or have you created a lifestyle that now requires you to make that much money? Why not consider ways to save money and cut down on expenses so that you can take a pay cut instead? The less you rely financially on your career the better, remember? And what about all the benefits you listed? The benefits of previous jobs do not have to be present in your next career. Just pick the ones that make a profound difference on your ability to be satisfied. To sum it up: Simplify your list and you'll improve your ability to find career happiness!

STEP 2: Next, you need to prioritize the list. Start with your Must-haves first and rank them in order of importance. Then, review your Nice-to-haves and Don't wants and rank those in order of preference as well. When you are done, you should have one long list of your career criteria in rank order. Complete this now.

With your Career Criteria List completed, you have in essence written an outline of your career goal. This outline is very important because it's going to help you achieve your Success Statement. Therefore, we'll need to make sure you've created an effective career goal. To do this, we need to test your Career Criteria List to make sure it has the "**A.M.P.**", or, in other words, the power it needs to help you.

Powering Up Your Career Goal

Over the years, I've recognized a clear pattern with regard to goal achievement. Besides making sure they wrote their goals down, my clients found it much easier to achieve their goals when the goal met three basic criteria. So I created an easy acronym that summarizes these guidelines. A.M.P. stands for:

Attainable
Measurable
Positive

While many people feel they are capable of setting a good goal, the reality is most people don't create goals that have all the necessary elements for success. Your Career Criteria List is your career goal. So it's important that we make sure you've defined criteria that meet the A.M.P. guidelines. Let's take a look at how a goal that follows the A.M.P. rules is more achievable.

Attainable

You may be thinking, "Well of course I've picked an attainable goal. Anything's possible if I put my mind to it." While it's true that anything we really set out to do should be achievable, there are still some things we need to consider.

For a goal to be attainable, it must be realistic. In other words, you should be able to achieve your goal in the time frame you've specified, using the resources and personal capacity available to you. Many times, people set goals that can ultimately be achieved, but are not realistic within the current situation. In other words, the goal is too large. The following is an example of an unrealistic career goal:

• I want to earn a starting salary $100,000 per year when I graduate from high school in three months. I only want to work 30 hours/week with a two-hour lunch break. The job should include full medical, dental and retirement benefits, as well as three-weeks paid vacation and unlimited sick days.

For the average individual, this goal is not realistic. At least not yet! Their knowledge base and experience level do not match the desired income and benefits. While this person could certainly work towards earning $100,000 per year, doing so out of high school with very little in the way of marketable skills makes this highly unlikely. There are exceptions to every rule, of course, and I encourage you to find them! But the better answer for most people is to revise the goal.

Although this as an obvious example, the point is that you need to test your goal to ensure it is attainable at this time. The best way to ensure your goal is realistic is to ask yourself the following questions:

• Can this goal be achieved in the time frame I have allotted?
• Is this goal something someone with my experience and knowledge base can achieve in the near future?
• Do I need to acquire any new skills or experience in order to achieve this goal?
• Are there any smaller goals I need to achieve first in order to reach this goal?

Breaking down your goal so it can be realistically achieved helps set yourself up for success. Take a moment to review your criterion list to make sure your career goal is realistic and thus, attainable.

Measurable

In order for any goal to be measurable, it must be well-defined. In other words, it must describe, in specific detail, what you want to accomplish. How else will you know if you've accomplished it? Seems simple enough, right? Let's test your ability to identify goals that are "specific." Place a check mark next to each of the career goals below you feel is specific:

- I want benefits.
- I want to make a good income.

Did you check either of them? I hope not! None of the goals above are specific. None of them outline what would need to be accomplished to claim victory. For example, what do you want for benefits? How much money is a "good income?"

The examples above don't provide enough definition from which to build a game plan for success. Goals that are specific allow us to break them down and work backward to set up action steps and milestones. Let's look at some goals that are specific:

- I want to find a new 9-5 job that offers 50% tuition reimbursement for college courses and is only 20 minutes from my home within the next three months.
- I want to make $40,000 per year in salary in the next six months.

The goals above offer the detail needed to outline our plan of attack. To guarantee your goals are specific enough to be measured, you must make sure your goal answers the following three questions:

1. What do you want to accomplish?
2. By how much?
3. By when?

Using numbers in your goal is very important. They help to gauge where you are in the process of achieving your goal. In other words, you will be able to *measure* your success against them. In addition to lacking specifics, many people fail to accurately define goals so they can be measured effectively. Let's test your knowledge again. Which of the following goals can be measured effectively?

- I want to earn 10% more than I do now.
- I want to earn $40,000.

They both have numbers to represent the goal to be achieved, so they must be measurable, right? But are they effective? Let's look at each one:

- Does 10% include benefits? What if you were given extra vacation pay or the company picked up a larger portion of your health insurance premium? If either of these changes equaled 10% more earnings, would you be happy?

- Would you be happy with $40,000/year if the job offered no benefits whatsoever? What would you have to pay out of pocket to cover your own benefits? Would $40,000 be sufficient still? Measurable means a goal so clearly defined; there is no doubt when the goal has been achieved.

Let's look at some improved examples of the two goals above:

- I want to increase my net or "take home" pay by $500 per month.
- I want to make $30,000/year with full dental, medical and retirement benefits paid by my employer for working 40 hours/week and earn two weeks paid vacation and at least 5 paid sick days each year.

There is no ambiguity in the goals above. We will be able to clearly determine when we have accomplished the goal, and there will be no question as to whether or not the goal was achieved in its entirety.

Can you see the importance of having a goal that is measurable? Take a moment now to re-write your Career Criteria List so that it is accurate and effective at providing a measurement for your success.

Now that you have designed a career goal that is both attainable and measurable, let's make sure it meets the final criterion: Positive.

Positive

Positive means that achievement of your goal will not adversely affect any of the other key areas of life. A goal is not positive if in the process of achieving it you can do harm to yourself, other people or the environment.

For example, the following goal is not positive:

- I want the highest paying job I can get and am willing to do whatever it takes, even if it means I won't see my family and friends the way I want to, or take care of my health the way I want to.

While you may earn your dream salary, should you achieve the goal above, it will come at a huge cost. Does it really make sense to negatively impact other key areas of your life to achieve your career goal? Remember your Core Values and how you ranked them? When other areas of life are sacrificed or compromised for the sake of a goal, then the goal should be reconsidered.

While the example above is extreme, many people still manage to create goals that are not positive. Are you guilty of creating goals that have the potential of negatively impacting other areas of your life? Goals set and reached in one area of your life should serve to help the other areas of your life. Let me provide you with a real-life example.

I have a friend whose father was determined to own his own business. He left his job as an insurance agent and started his own agency. He did very well and was able to build the business up so that it provided well for him and his family while at the same time giving him the professional freedom and challenge he desired.

Soon after, my friend's father set another goal: To be the biggest insurance agency in the state. It was an ambitious goal. And while it appeared to be both attainable and measurable, it was not positive. In order to achieve this goal, my friend's father had to work twice as many hours and travel almost every week. He rarely saw his family and his wife. He was tired all the time and was unable to take care of himself. He didn't eat well and had no time to exercise. On the weekends, he was so busy catching up on his work at home that he was unable to relax or spend time with his family. Eventually, my friend's father achieved his goal. Unfortunately, by the time he achieved it, he was divorced, had no relationship with his children, had no hobbies, very few friends, was overweight, drank too much and was told by his doctor he was a candidate for a heart attack. Was his goal positive? No. Too many other areas of his life and the life of others were negatively affected. Remember the Life Balance Grid? To ensure a goal is positive, ask yourself the following questions:

- Am I asking for too much from my goal?
- Will I need to compromise or make sacrifices in other areas of my life that will negatively impact my overall happiness in order to achieve this goal?
- Will other people be negatively affected by my attempt to reach this goal?

Keep your goals positive and you'll keep them attainable. Take a moment now to re-write your career criteria in your notebook using what you've learned about the A.M.P. guidelines.

Ah-ha Moment: The A.M.P. guidelines can also be used to help improve the effectiveness and attainability of all your life goals. Remember the Success Statements you created for the eight key areas of life? How many of the statements you recorded in your notebook do you think meet the A.M.P. guidelines? Take a moment to see if your Success Statements are attainable, measurable and positive. You'll be surprised at how much better you could be defining success for each key area of your life. The more specific you can be with regard to your Success Statements, the better the chances that you'll actually achieve them. The goal is to find satisfaction through life balance; true success is when all your life goals work in harmony. To do that, you'll need to define them as accurately and effectively as possible. So power up your Success Statements today with the help of the A.M.P. guidelines!

Now that you've created a more powerful and effective Career Criteria List using the A.M.P. guidelines, you'll use it, along with your PSP Summary Sheet, to help you find the ideal career for you!

Career Tests

Keeping what you've learned about yourself and your career goals in mind, it's time to start looking at the vast array of careers available to you. So where do you begin? This is the one area in which I have not bothered to develop my own tools. Why? Because there so many wonderful tools already developed, I saw no use in creating another one. One such example is an assessment tool created by the University of Missouri's Career Center. It is called the Career Interests Game and you can find it at www.career.missouri.edu. This test is the copyrighted work of the **University of Missouri's Career Center**. It uses the RIASEC model of occupations, which is the copyrighted work of **Dr. John L. Holland** and his publisher, **Psychological Assessment Resources, Inc. (PAR)**.

The Career Interests Game is based on Dr. John Holland's theory that people and work environments can be loosely classified into six different groups. Different peoples' personalities may find different environments more to their liking. While you may have some interests in and similarities to several of the six groups, you may be attracted primarily to two or three of the areas. These two or three letters are your Holland Code. This test asks you to rank, based upon a brief description of each, six possible categories that interest you. They are as follows:

Investigative
Artistic
Social
Realistic
Enterprising
Conventional

Once you have prioritized the list, you can look at the top three to determine your Holland Code. The website enables you to click on each of the categories in order to see a list of common traits for this work type and a list of jobs that are a match for this category.

What I find particularly exciting is that each job has a Holland Code next to it. So I advise clients to look at the career lists for each of their top three categories and identify all jobs that have at least two, if not all three of their top three categories in the Holland Code attached to it. From there, clients can rank in order of preference all of the jobs on this master list that they find of interest. Another element of this test I find helpful is the descriptions attached to each job listed. You can select any job to make the U.S. Labor Department's current description for that job appear. This enables you to learn more about any career you find interesting.

Most importantly, I find the categories Dr. Holland has identified help to reinforce what you've learned about yourself so far. Given all the work you've done to identify your personal strengths and unique career goals, you should find it very easy to interpret why you chose your top three categories in Dr. Holland's model!

This is just one example of the multitude of tools available to help you research and identify careers that interest you. The key to effectively using resources like The University of Missouri's Career Center Career Interest Game is simple: When completing this or any career interest test, be sure to review your PSP Summary Sheet and Career Criteria List often to see how your various styles and preferences may or may not support each career option. As you drill down and look at each job you find interesting in greater detail, ask yourself this question, "Could this job support my career goals and make good use of my unique strengths?" In other words, select careers that have the greatest chance of making you happy!

Take some time now to check out The University of Missouri's Career Center Career Interest Game and any other tests you think might be helpful. Some of the major job resource websites, such as www.monster.com, www.careerbuilder.com and www.hotjobs.com offer career interest tools. You can also search the web by completing key word searches that include the words "free career tests" to help you. If you find that the free tests aren't providing you with enough options, you can always try a fee-based test as well.

Your goal is to identify the top ten careers that interest you right now. Once you have recorded them in your notebook, you can move on to the next step: Ranking their ability to meet your needs.

Ah-ha Moment: Researching careers is your opportunity to dream. Don't hold back from identifying any and all jobs that really excite you. You should not eliminate any job from your initial list because you feel it "isn't respectable" or "it isn't feasible right now." Let the process decide that for you. There will be plenty of time to evaluate a career's current viability in the next section. For now, you need to imagine that if all the jobs in the world were equal (similar pay, benefits, training, hours, location, etc.), which job would you find the most interesting and fulfilling? Finding career satisfaction comes from your ability to stop imposing limitations on yourself. Let yourself finally explore all of the careers you are drawn to but never thought were possible. Who knows what variation of the job could be developed to fit your needs?

Career Matrix

It's time to put the pieces of the puzzle together. Each career you have identified will have strengths and weaknesses with regard to its ability to meet your unique needs. Here is an example of a table I have my clients use to facilitate this process. Take a moment now to create a similar table in your notebook. First, list all of the careers you selected in the column provided. Then, rate each career against the career criteria you've identified. You will need to change and/or add to the criteria listed across the top so that they reflect your own Career Criteria List. The goal is for you to have, at the very least, all of your "Must-haves" listed across the top and then as many of the other criteria listed as you see fit. For each criterion, you will need to create point values to represent the level in which a career could provide that criterion. Once you have listed the necessary criteria and corresponding point values, you can review each career listed and determine the score it should receive for each criterion. Finally, tally your scores to find the careers with the greatest ability to provide you with long-term career satisfaction.

	Career Additional Education or Training Not Needed – 3 Some Needed – 2 Required – 1	Hours/Days Worked Low – 3 Moderate – 2 High – 1	Transfer-able Skills Between Careers High – 5 Moderate – 3 Low – 1	Salary & Benefits High – 3 Moderate – 2 Low – 1	Use of "Unique Gift" High – 5 Moderate – 3 Low – 1	Location Close/Flexible – 3 Moderate – 2 Far/Inflexible – 1	TOTAL SCORE
1.							
2.							
3.							
4.							
5.							
6.							
7.							
8.							
9.							
10.							

NOTE: Your point values for each of the career criteria should be based upon their importance and value to you. For example, any of your "Must-have" criteria should have higher point values than your "Nice-to-haves" and "Don't-wants." Why? They weigh more heavily on your decision. You should add or subtract points in order to factor each criterion in appropriately. For example, I have listed Transferable Skills and Use of Your Unique Gift with higher point values in the example table because of their impact on job satisfaction. However, if other criteria (i.e. Salary, Benefits, etc.) also have a large impact on your career satisfaction, their point values should be raised as well to reflect your personal preference. Take a moment now to complete your own Career Matrix in your notebook.

The Results

How did you do? Are you surprised by your results or does the list just confirm your suspicions? What are your feelings about the top choice? How about the top three choices?

At this point, you might think I'll insist you select the top point-earning career and start job hunting, but you're wrong. There is one more thing you need to do. Use your heart! Which career do you feel most excited about? If you followed the instructions carefully and were honest with the point ratings, then your first choice should be in the top three. If it is, then go for it! Just because a career ranks the highest doesn't mean that the second or third place winners are out of the picture.

This process serves to help you put a logical perspective on a sometimes illogical area of life: Your career. But no matter how many tests and tools you use, the final decision comes down to you. Pick the career that your gut tells you will give you the greatest level of satisfaction and excitement. In other words, use these tools as your foundation for narrowing down your choices and making an informed decision, but ultimately, you need to rely on the best tool of all: Intuition. Have you determined a career direction? Do you know what you want to do next? Good, then let's move on and identify what it's going to take to find it.

Ah-ha Moment: One of the hottest trends in career development these days is the "hobby-turned-career" concept. It's the idea of developing a hobby that can eventually be transitioned into a full-time career. Recognizing that our career interests will most likely change over our lifetime, some people are taking a proactive approach to transitioning their careers by developing their next career while they are still working in the current one. I have recommended this to several of my clients, especially, if they find they get bored easily and need a lot of variety in their career. I have clients begin by reviewing the careers that ranked high on their Career Matrix but didn't make the final cut. Once identified, they ask themselves the following questions with respect to each one:

- Could some aspect of this career be done in my spare time?
- Does this career offer a creative outlet I could focus on in my spare time?
- Does this career require additional education or experience I could obtain in my spare time?
- Would I find this career particularly fun to do in my spare time?

If you can answer 'yes' to three or more of these questions for any of the careers listed, you may have found a great hobby-turned-career option for you.

While this concept is not for everyone, for those individuals who can and want to develop a paying hobby, the long-term career benefits are excellent.

Not only have you found something fun to do in your spare time, but should something happen in your existing career, (i.e. you get laid off or are just plain ready to leave), you have an automatic back-up plan!

PART III

THE G.L.O.W. METHOD: Own Your Actions

STEP #3: Own Your Actions

Opportunity is missed by most people because it is dressed in overalls and looks like work.—Thomas A. Edison

While you might think the hard work is over, the truth is, it's just begun. You've identified a career goal and are ready to find your next job. Great work, but you still need to make that goal a reality. The "Own Your Actions" step helps you get over the common roadblocks people encounter when trying to achieve their goals.

In this step, you are taking an inventory of what you'll need, both physically and mentally, to reach your goal. As you can imagine, this next phase of the process is where many people fall down. Why? Because while many people know what they want to achieve with respect to their goal, they:

A) Don't have the right tools and resources.
B) Don't have the right mind-set.

The following pages address these issues with respect to career goals. We will begin by putting together a key tool used in the job hunting process: Your resumé.

Resumés

One of the first things people ask you when you say you are looking for a job is, "Do you have a resumé?" I remember the first time I put a resumé together. I couldn't imagine having enough valuable experience to fill a page. So what did I do? I tried to make myself look as good as possible by describing, in great detail, each of my accomplishments. I ended up with a wordy, confusing, useless piece of paper. Yet, I used it! Yes, I had no idea that my resumé was ineffective. It wasn't until several years later when I started hiring employees that I realized the real purpose and value of a good resumé.

Creating A Powerful Resumé

For a resumé to be powerful, it needs to be three things:

- Easy to read.
- Simple to assess.
- Appropriate for any career.

Let me provide more detail regarding each of these important resumé criteria.

Making A Resumé Easy To Read: An Experience Outline

A powerful resumé needs to be written in a format and font that enables an employer to quickly scan the resumé for key pieces of information. When potential employers look at your resumé for the first time, they will also be making their first impressions about you. If your resumé is verbose, an employer might assume the same about you. If it is visually busy and hard to follow, the employer may feel you might be that way, too. Simple fonts and concise words are the key to a powerful resumé. The phrase, "less is more" certainly applies to resumés. If your resumé is clear, succinct and well-formatted, potential employers will take away a great first impression.

So how do you ensure your resumé is easy to read? You must take the time to organize your information as accurately and concisely as possible. Grab your notebook, because here is a simple process for creating what I like to call your "Experience Outline."

Experience Outline

1   Make a chronological list of all your work experiences, including internships and volunteer work, listing job titles, company names, locations and dates of employment.

     a. List only key job responsibilities and achievements.

     b. Start each description with a verb that summarizes the action you took to achieve each task (e.g. managed, created, developed, assisted, etc.).

     c. You should have no more than four bullets points for each job, and each bullet point should fit on one line.

     d. Eliminate any industry lingo or terminology from each bullet. Use general terms that anyone from any industry could understand.

2.   Make a chronological list of all your educational experiences listing degrees and certificates earned, schools or programs attended, dates of completion and areas of concentration.

     a. Add excellence awards, participation in school programs and any other contributions as bullet points, keeping them short with no more than four bullets for each one.

3.   Identify a list of all software programs or technologies you are familiar with as well as any other unique areas of experience (e.g. extensive charity work where you held actual positions, a well-developed hobby where you've made notable achievements, and any awards or other certificates of achievement you've been given personally for your efforts) and group them by category.

     a. You should have short bullet points with no more than three for each category.

Once this data is outlined, you can move on to creating the most important part of a powerful resumé: The Experience Summary.

Making A Resumé Simple To Assess: The Experience Summary

What is an Experience Summary? It is a brief section at the top of a resumé, (just after your contact information), that lists your experience in a quantifiable and strategic fashion. Why is it important? Because the Experience Summary enables a potential employer to quickly assess your skills and achievements to determine your viability as a candidate. In effect, the experience summary saves the potential employer the hassle of having to read through your resumé with a fine-tooth comb in order to figure out if you have the basic skills for the job. Employers love the Experience Summary. It is eye-catching and helpful. If you want to stand out and look good, you need an Experience Summary. So how do you create one? The following steps can help you put together an effective Experience Summary:

1. Using the information you outlined in the previous exercise, take a moment now to add up the total years of experience you have for each of the following skill sets. Be sure to really consider each work experience, identifying as many skills used as possible.

    a. Management
    b. Project Management
    c. Sales
    d. Marketing
    e. Research & Development
    f. Finance & Accounting
    g. Operations
    h. Training
    i. Customer Service

2. Identify any unique skills not listed above and total up the years of experience you have for each as well. (e.g. Equipment Operation, Construction, Trade Skills such as Plumbing, etc.)

3. List all the industries in which you have experience.

4. List all the degrees and certifications you have earned.

5. If applicable, list all the technologies in which you are experienced.

Great! You have just put together the crucial information needed to showcase your experience. Now it's time to put it all together into a fantastic, one-page resumé.

Making A Resumé Appropriate For Any Employer: "New & Improved" Resumé Formats

Some of the most valuable tools I've designed for my clients are two "new and improved" formats for creating a resumé. As I mentioned earlier, once I started hiring employees, it became quite clear to me that the traditional resumé design no longer worked for the majority of today's employees. Why? Because each person's skills and abilities and the paths they've taken to achieve them are too diverse.

Additionally, recognizing today's fast-paced rate in which we gain more skills and experience, a new format needed to be developed which could be easily and consistently updated without losing its effectiveness.

Therefore, I took it upon myself to design two resumé formats. The first format is for anyone who is new to the working world and feels they have less experience and education than the average employee. For example, if you had trouble adding up years of experience for the different skill sets listed in the previous section, or you have less than two years experience in any or all of the categories, this format is for you. I call it the "Entry Level" format. The second format is for anyone who has been in the workforce for at least two or more years and feels they have some quantifiable experience. If you were able to list a fair amount of years of experience for more than four of the skills listed above, this format is for you. I call this the "Advanced" format. Which ever one you choose, one thing is certain: These formats will help you put real value on the skills and abilities you have. Let's take a look at each resumé format.

Resumé Format #1 – Entry Level

This resumé doesn't require you to put years of experience next to your skill sets. Take a look at the example provided:

James Monroe
111 Salem Street, Smithtown, NY 11111
Phone: (555) 331-7345 Email: jmsssny@xyz.com

EXPERIENCE SUMMARY

Work Skills: Customer Service/Problem Resolution
Office Operations
Staff Management & Training
Inventory Management
Restaurant Operations
Landscape Design/Maintenance

Degrees: BA – Philosophy/Psychology
PC Skills: MS Word, PowerPoint, Internet Research

EMPLOYMENT

Landscaper   2003 - Present
XYZ Landscaping, Jones, NY
- ⊙ Implemented landscape designs.
- ⊙ Executed plant maintenance.
- ⊙ Used machinery to support efforts.

Office Assistant   1999-2004
Dugan, Inc., Smithville, NY
- ⊙ Provided extensive customer service.
- ⊙ Coordinated internal communication.
- ⊙ Responded to problems.

Shift Manager   1996-1999
Appleton's Restaurant, Smithville, NY
- ⊙ Trained employees.
- ⊙ Calculated inventory.
- ⊙ Managed operations.

EDUCATION & HONORS

Bachelor of Arts, Cum Laude May (2003)
Southern Connecticut State University, New Haven, CT
Major: Philosophy **Minor:** Psychology **G.P.A. 3.6**
- ⊙ Dean's List – All 8 semesters
- ⊙ 2003 Forrest H. Peterson Award for Excellence in Philosophy
- ⊙ Psi Chi National Society in Psychology
- ⊙ Zeta Delta Epsilon Honor-Service Society
- ⊙ Golden Key Honor Society

In this resumé example the person has great work skills, but not enough years of experience to list them. As this candidate continues to grow his skills over time, he will not only be able to add years of experience, but he will be able to pare down his bullet points for each of the current listings in order to make room for the additional experiences that will need to be added.

Here is another example of the Entry Level resumé format:

Jerry Barns
110 Blanford Street, Chatham, VA 00211
Phone: (555)114-4669 E-mail: jbarns@xyz.com

EXPERIENCE SUMMARY

R.E. Appraisal, Construction & Demolition
Peer Mentoring, Coaching & Teaching
Non-profit Association - Participation & Management
Restaurant Service Operations

EMPLOYMENT

General Laborer, DVD Inc., Chatham, VA   June – Nov. 2004
- ⊙ Selectively demolished portions of commercial buildings.
- ⊙ Maintained a clear working environment.

Busser, Bourbon Steak House, Stenford, VA   Summer 2000
- ⊙ Cleared eating areas.
- ⊙ Stocked & maintained bar supplies.

Demolition & Construction Laborer, BK Construction, Bay, VA   Summer 2000
- ⊙ Dismantled & removed unusable materials from site.
- ⊙ Properly disposed of debris & assisted in construction.

EDUCATION & CERTIFICATIONS

Bachelor of Arts, Quinten College, New London, VA (May 2004)
Major: History, Society & Culture *Minor:* Psychology
- ⊙ V.P. of Club Ice Hockey Program
- ⊙ Teacher's Assistant
- ⊙ Tenant Council Representative
- ⊙ Assistant Lacrosse Coach
- ⊙ Dormitory Proctor/Resident Assistant

Bartenders School of America
- ⊙ Certificate of Achievement

KKR R.E. Academy, Certificates of Completion:
- ⊙ Basics of R.E. Appraisal
- ⊙ Uniform Standards of Professional Appraisal Practice
- ⊙ Appraising 1-4 Family Properties

AWARDS & COMMUNITY SERVICE

⊙ Academic & Personal Development Award, New Hampton School
⊙ Multiple Sports Honors - MVP, Most Improved & Captain's
⊙ Community Beautification Volunteer (i.e. lawn & building maintenance)

In this resumé example, the candidate's skills are less traditional. He also doesn't have enough years of experience to make it worthwhile to list. The approach here is to highlight the uniqueness of his skills by creating categories that summarize both the skills and industries he had worked in.

Notice that while each resumé has a little different format with respect to fonts and the use of lines to separate sections, each is clean and simple. The Experience Summary at the top of each one is boldface to add extra emphasis and to draw the eye directly to it. Both of these individuals will find it easy to add information to this format as they gain more experience, especially, if they do so by following the "Advanced" resumé format.

Resumé Format #2 – Advanced

This next resumé format can help even the most complicated and diverse person put their skills and abilities on a single page. By using the Experience Summary to showcase the breadth and depth of your skills, you will be able to condense what is written in the sections beneath it. Let's take a look at an example:

Amanda L. Kirkland

34 Mainland Drive, Albany, TN 10222
E-mail: alkirkland@xyz.com Phone: (555) 884-9876

EXPERIENCE SUMMARY

Project Management – 12 yrs.   **Training & Customer Support – 12 yrs.**
Sales – 8+ yrs.   **Operations – 8+ yrs.**

Industries – Information Technology, Financial, Insurance, Consulting

CERTIFICATIONS & TECHNOLOGIES

APB Certified Internetworking Engineer
- Routing and Switching, 1997 (CCIE #3062), Voice Technologies, 2003 (written only)

Call Center & VoIP Protocols
- IVR/VRU, ACD and Call Routing
- SIP, H.323, MGCP, SCCP

Routing Protocols, Multicast & System Automation
- BGP, OSPF, EIRGP, RIP
- PIM, DVMRP, MBGP
- ALERT, OASYS

WORK HISTORY

Consulting Systems Engineer – APB Systems, Inc. Albany, TN   **JUL 2002–Present**
- ⊙ Top Northeast Sales Engineer for VoIP technology; "System Engineer of the Region" in 2000 & 2003.
- ⊙ Responsible for $5M in direct sales and $10+M in support sales.
- ⊙ Designed and implemented technology demonstration room, resulting in $7+M in new sales.
- ⊙ Mentored customers, channel partners and resellers on technology "best practices."

Systems Engineer – APB Systems, Inc. Albany, TN   **JUL 1996–JUN 2002**
- ⊙ Designed and implemented complex computer networks throughout the Northeast.
- ⊙ Technical specialist for the financial industry.
- ⊙ Lead sales engineer on one of Cisco's largest implementations for major N.E. financial company.
- ⊙ Provided technical marketing function for sales force, including development of sales proposals.

Integration Consultant – Timland Financial Services, Albany, TN   **DEC 1992–JUN 1996**
- ⊙ Developed interfaces to financial database and messaging system.
- ⊙ Trained and supported internal and external clients.
- ⊙ Advised clients on system design and product features.

EDUCATION

B.S., Grey University – Chemistry Major, Computer Science Minor (1992)

We can see in this resumé that the candidate has a solid amount of experience in several skill sets. Moreover, her extensive knowledge of specific technologies is very impressive. Even if she chose to leave her current field all together to pursue a different career direction, this resumé shows how transferable her skills are to other careers. Let's look at a slightly different version of the Advanced resumé format:

Ellen T. Margolis

141 West Road, Martin, FL 00999
Phone: (555) 099-3373 E-mail: emargolis@xyz.com

EXPERIENCE SUMMARY

Project Management – 8+ yrs.   **Operations – 7+ yrs.**   **Finance – 8+ yrs.**
Staff Management – 4+ yrs.   **Sales – 2 yrs.**   **Marketing – 2 yrs.**

Degrees – MBA, B.S. – Management, B.S. – Marketing
Industries – Real Estate, Consumer Services, Web Marketing

WORK HISTORY

Associate Director – First R.E. International, New York, NY   **1998-2001**
- Managed $100+ million commercial assets portfolio.
- Responsible for all elements of asset management.
- Handled management of property and leasing staffs, financial analysis and reporting, and development of business plans.
- Assisted in investment targeting, pricing, evaluation, acquisition, supervising of loan compliance and refinancing options.

Sr. Commercial Asset Manager – ESTEN Financial, Martin, FL   **1996-1998**
- Managed $40 million portfolio of non-performing commercial mortgages and REO properties.
- Achieved over $15 million in book gain for the corporation.
- Responsible for determining, negotiation and implementing most desirable resolutions.
- Maximized Net Operating Income and increased market value via successful property management.

Loan Resolution Specialist – ESTEN Financial, Martin, FL   **1994-1996**
- Managed $20 million portfolio of over 200 residential non performing mortgages and REO properties.
- Performed financial analysis on non-performing assets.
- Determined most beneficial resolution for mortgager.
- Prepared required documentation for successful completion of foreclosure process.

EDUCATION

MBA, Byron School of Business, Devlin College – Derby, MA   **2001-2003**
- Kellerman Entrepreneurial Internship Program (KEIP) participant.
- Created strategic growth plan for Com, Inc., an online marketing company.
- Devlin Consulting Alliance Program participant.
- Completed academically based, year-long team consulting project for real estate division of Finley Investments.

B.S., Management & B.S., Marketing, Stevens College – Smithfield, FL **1989-1993**

In this resumé, the candidate's practical experience while getting their MBA was added to the overall years of experience to showcase an even broader set of skills.

Like many people, this person has been in the same career and industry for their entire work experience. Yet, by analyzing their experience in terms of transferable skills, we see a depth and breadth of experience that could clearly be useful in any industry.

No matter which resumé format you choose, the key is to create an Experience Summary that conveys as much about your diversity as an employee as possible. Quantifying your skills and summarizing your knowledge will make a big difference in your ability to explore new careers.

Take time now to create your own "New and Improved" resumé. You'll be amazed at just how much great experience you have! Now let's move on to another important job hunting tool: Your Career Story.

Ah-ha Moment: After all the hard work you've put in to creating your "New and Improved" resumé, don't forget that the little things can make all the difference. Here's a checklist to ensure you are putting your best foot forward:

1) Keep it to one page, no matter what! – If your resumé is running long, go back and look where you can edit. Less is more. You will always be able to explain your experience in greater detail during an interview.

2) Fonts have a huge impact. – Make sure your font is no smaller than 10 points and no larger than 12 points. Use fonts with clean lines that are easy on the eyes (i.e. Arial, Tahoma). Use bold text to highlight only the most important parts, (i.e. Experience Summary, job titles, etc.), and avoid using italics text as much as possible.

3) Be honest! – Don't change or omit data to make yourself look better. Tell the truth about gaps in employment (everyone has them). Why give yourself the added stress of having to remember the "white lies" you've put down on paper. Tell the truth and be proud of who you are. Honesty and pride are traits all good employers value.

Use these tips to ensure your hard work is not overlooked because of some trivial mistakes. You deserve to find the best job for you. Missing out on the perfect opportunity because of some resumé blunders would be a real disappointment.

Career Story

A Career Story is a short story you can use to help you find your next job. What is this story about? It's a story about you and your search to find a career path that brings you greater happiness and satisfaction.

The work you have done up to this point has taken you on a sort of journey. You have done a lot of personal development and hopefully have had a lot of Ah-ha Moments. In other words, you have changed as a person. This is an exciting story.

People, especially employers, like to hear how individuals have grown and where this growth has led them. In your case, it's toward a new outlook and direction for your career. This is the story you need to tell as you search for your new job. This story will excite and captivate potential employers. Why? Every good employer wants to find and help employees who are willing to put the time and commitment into discovering what they were meant to do.

So how do you develop your story? Imagine you are meeting with a person who has the ability to get you your dream job. The only thing you have to do is describe to her how you arrived at the realization that this was the career for you. So how did you figure this out, by accident or luck? Of course not! Look at all the work you have just completed in an effort to clarify your career direction. You've assessed some very personal things in order to gain a clearer perspective of your unique situation. It's time to share your insight with those who can help you achieve your goal.

Career Story Exercise

Step 1: Fill in the Blanks

To help you put your Career Story together, I've developed a "fill in the blanks" tool. Take a moment now to complete the exercise below by adding in the information as needed.

Hello, my name is _____.

I'm in the process of making a career change and was wondering if you would be able to help me?

I recently did some in-depth self analysis and have determined that a career in _____ would make the best use of my potential and help me achieve my personal and professional goals.

In particular, I learned that both my _____ style and my _____ preference really lend themselves to this career. Coupled with my _____ experience and my interest in _____, I'm confident I'd be both highly productive and happy in this kind of job.

I'm looking to spend some time with individuals in similar positions so I can learn more about what it takes to be successful in this type of career, as well as the best methods for getting into the field. Would you be able to help me, or could you recommend someone who might be able to help me?

Step 2: Put it in Your Own Words

Once you've filled in the blanks, you are ready to make this story your very own. Take a moment to read through the story and then re-write it in your notebook to reflect the same information in your own words. Use language that reflects your own style and manner of speaking. Keep re-reading and adjusting your story, adding or changing information as needed, until it encapsulates as honestly and accurately as possible how you have arrived at this point in your career search. Is it all done? Good, then it's time to test your Career Story.

Informational Interviews - The Ultimate Career Story Test

You will be able to test and perfect your Career Story by using it as your introduction when you call to set up your first Informational Interview. One thing I suggest every client do before they embark full steam in pursuit of a new career, is to complete at least one, if not more, of what is known as Informational Interviews.

Unlike traditional job interviews where employers contact you to come in and meet them regarding an open position, Informational Interviews involve you contacting individuals whose career paths are similar to the one you wish to pursue so that you can meet with them to learn more about their careers and what it takes to be successful at them. I have my clients do this for two reasons:

1. It offers them an opportunity to confirm that the day-to-day elements of the career they are pursuing are consistent with their own visions of what working in this field is like.

2. It's a simple way to connect with members of your chosen field who can help point you in the right direction with regard to job opportunities. The beauty of Informational Interviews is they're beneficial to both parties. As the interviewer, you will get valuable information and potentially develop a professional relationship with someone that might be able to help you find a job. At the same time, the interviewee gets an opportunity to help another colleague by sharing their own personal story of success. Moreover, there is no pressure in the situation. A job is not up for grabs. This meeting is strictly for information gathering purposes only. There is nothing to be "lost" as a result of this interview. Now you might be thinking, "Sure, an Informational Interview sounds great, but what if

no one will meet with me?" How do I know people will meet you for an Informational Interview? People love giving advice and perspective. When you ask individuals for an Informational Interview, you are in essence telling them you respect and admire their career accomplishments. Who wouldn't be excited about meeting to discuss how they achieved their success?

In short, Informational Interviews are one of the best methods for finding a job. Make a good impression, and who knows what doors could be opened for you? I've had many clients get new jobs as a result of Informational Interviews. The people they met were kind enough to forward their resumés to key decision makers and, in some cases, even set up additional Information Interviews with hiring managers. These actions helped my clients land their dream jobs. While I can't guarantee the same results for you, I can assure you that the more Informational Interviews you do, the more certain you will be about your career choice, and the easier time you will have finding out the best and quickest way to get a job in your chosen field.

Who Do I Contact?

The easiest way to start setting up Informational Interviews is to put the word out to family and friends that you are looking to have this kind of meeting with someone in your field of interest. Most of the time, somebody knows someone you can talk to.

If you don't have any immediate prospects, then it's time to contact a company that employs people in the role you are interested in. I suggest contacting receptionists and sharing your Career Story with them. Receptionists are friendly, outgoing, helpful people by nature. Most of the time, they can direct you to the person in their company that can help you. If the receptionist can't help you, then I suggest asking to speak to someone in the Human Resources department. Or, if it is a smaller company, with no HR staff I suggest asking to speak directly with the owner. These individuals should be able to identify who in their organization could speak with you. The goal is to meet in-person, or at least over the phone, for no more than a ? hour. Your agenda is simple. You will be asking this person's opinion of the following:

1. How did they successfully attain the position they are in now?
2. What does it take for a person to be successful in this type of career?
3. If they were in your shoes, what steps would they take to land a job in this field?

Don't be afraid to mention these meeting objectives in your efforts to set up the Informational Interview. The more the people you are contacting understand why you want to speak with them, the easier it is for them to say 'yes' to meeting with you.

While not every person you contact will be willing to get together with you, I think you will be pleasantly surprised at the number of people who are willing to lend a hand via an Informational Interview.

Ah-ha Moment: When setting up and completing Informational Interviews, many of the same protocols from traditional interviewing apply. Here is a short list of things you should remember to do to ensure you make the most of your interviewing efforts:

1) Be prepared. - Have your list of questions ready as well as a hard copy of your resumé in the event the interviewee would like to take one to a colleague or hiring manager for review.

2) Be on time. – You requested this interview, so don't be late! Arrive at least 10-15 minutes early to ensure you will not waste any of the interviewee's time.

3) Listen carefully. – This is your chance to learn as much as you can. Don't spend too much time talking about yourself. Aside from sharing with the interviewee a basic overview regarding your situation, use this time to let them speak. The more they share the better.

4) Dress appropriately. – Make a good first impression by dressing up for the meeting. Clean, unwrinkled clothes are a must. While you don't need to over-dress, be sure not to under-dress for the meeting either. Show your respect by dressing accordingly.

5) Send thank you e-mails. – These days, a thank you e-mail has replaced the standard thank you note. It enables you to send your thanks on the very same day as your meeting. Be sure to thank the interviewee not only for their time, but for the valuable insights they shared, making note of at least one piece of information in particular. Convey your thanks by citing specifically the key items you learned from the interviewee. This will also show how well you listened to what they had to say!

6) Follow-up as directed. – If the interviewee offers you a lead on a job or refers you to someone else for an interview, pursue these items immediately and then let the interviewee know of your progress via e-mail. Show your appreciation and respect for their kindness by being prompt and thorough. This will serve to make a good impression on the interviewee, making it more likely they will feel comfortable referring you again. By following these rules, you will be sure to make the most of your Informational Interviewing opportunities!

Other Job Hunting Methods

In my opinion, Informational Interviewing is the best way to find your next job, particularly, if you are making a radical career change. However, there are other ways of job hunting that can and should be used in conjunction with your Informational Interviews to help expedite your search. Let's take a look at a few of them now.

Staffing Agencies

One of the most under-appreciated methods for transitioning to a new career is through the use of a staffing agency. Also known as temporary agencies, these companies specialize in providing short-term help to a large number of companies across a wide range of industries. Unfortunately, many people don't consider this option because of an outdated stigma attached to the temporary industry. Some people feel that these agencies are for people who are "under-employable," in other words, people who can't get a job on their own. This is the furthest thing from the truth. These days, 95% of companies have used or plan to use a staffing service to provide them with some additional employees. The value to these companies is the opportunity to supplement their workforce to meet changing demands in their business. The advantage to you is the opportunity to work at a variety of companies in a variety of positions to see what you enjoy. The best part is that when the company and the employee feel they are a good fit for one another, the result is often a job offer of permanent employment. Once you've submitted your resumé to a staffing company, they will generally have you in for an interview to determine if they can find you the kind of work you are looking for. This will be your opportunity to share all that you've learned about yourself and the career path you've chosen. Staffing companies are highly responsive to those individuals who have a clear understanding of what they are looking for in their career. They can often have you working with in just a week or two of meeting with them! You can find a list of staffing companies in your local area phone book. Just pick up the phone and be ready to share your Career Story.

Web Sites

By far the most common job hunting method these days is the Internet. There's no faster way to feel like you are making an effort to find a new job than to post your resumé and surf the pages of job opportunities listed on any number of major job sites. The challenge with this method is that it's like finding a needle in a haystack. While you may submit your resumé to hundreds of jobs, you must remember that hundreds of other people are doing the very same thing. Who is reading all of these resumés? Probably a very overworked and overwhelmed hiring manager who is most likely just skimming each resumé to see if the skills listed are a perfect match. In other words, you won't stand out unless your resumé shows you are exactly what they are looking for. That said, should you skip posting your resumé and surfing the net? No. I'm a firm believer in using every resource available, and there is one advantage to this process: You can keep track of who's hiring in your industry of choice and can use that information to try to contact them directly in order to set up an Informational Interview. What better place to try to complete an Informational Interview than a place you know is actively hiring? So go ahead and use the web, just be realistic in your expectations as to what it can do for you. While you might get lucky, the majority of folks do not find their next job on a web site. In order to improve your chances of getting a response from a company posting jobs on the web, I suggest two things. First, be sure to post your resumé as outlined in the previous section. The Experience Summary is an eye-catching format that will make your resumé stand out on-line. Second, in the section that offers you an opportunity to write a few words to the hiring manager, be sure to write in a short version of your Career Story. This compelling summary will also serve as a unique feature and bring attention to you as a focused and motivated candidate for hire. By using these two tools, you will be sending a consistent message regarding your desire to find a job that fits your unique skills, abilities and personal preferences.

Job Fairs

Job Fairs are one-day events in which a large group of hiring companies come together to meet potential employees. These venues are held in big event halls where the companies can set up booths to host their materials and spend time speaking with potential candidates. These events are heavily advertised and offer individuals looking for work a great way to get face-to-face with lots of hiring managers. Think of it as a multitude of short Informational Interviews. Should an employer determine you might be a good fit for their company, they will set up a follow-up interview for you at their facility before you leave. Talk about an easy way to get your job search going. All you need is a stack of resumés, a notebook and pen, and you're ready to go. A couple of tips if you plan to attend one of these events: First, look your best. Each employer will be looking to see how much energy you put into presenting yourself. Clothes should be neat, clean and appropriate for the career you are seeking. Second, be ready to answer a range of questions about yourself. Review your resumé and think through what you want to convey to employers about your career search before you attend. Last, follow through with all the leads that you collect. Record the name and e-mail address of each person you speak with, or better yet, simply grab their business card. That way, you'll have the ability to send them a thank you e-mail as well as follow up with them in the event you want to set an Informational Interview. This kind of attention to detail makes a great impression.

Internships/Volunteering

I suggest this method to candidates who have no experience in their desired field. Don't be mistaken in thinking that you can't volunteer or do an internship because you need a full-time, paying position. Internships and volunteer work can be done in as little time as once or twice a month. If you are willing to offer your time and services for free, I guarantee you will find someone willing to take you up on your offer. I think this is a particularly great method for trying out a new career.

You will get work experience and a chance to see if the career is what you thought it would be. With just a small investment in time, you could avoid making a big career mistake. The reality is that no matter how exciting a career sounds to you, and no matter how strong a match it is for you on paper, the actual job just might not work for you in real life. Wouldn't it be good to find that out before you leaped into the career full-time? Getting an internship or setting up some volunteer work is simple. All you need to do is start calling various companies and people in the field you have chosen to get the word out that you are looking to work for free. Have your resumé ready and be prepared to do a short interview. While most places will happily take on free help, they will want to make sure that your intentions are good and that you will at least be capable of making a contribution to the organization. Finally, the best thing you bring to an internship or volunteer work is a positive attitude. Be excited, helpful and proactive. Focus on learning as much as you can. Observe closely. Take notes. Do whatever you can to make the most of your experience. Why? Because making a great impression while interning or volunteering can lead to potential job offers. Prove yourself now and your employer just may decide to hire you, or at least help you find a job in the field.

Professional Associations

Almost all professions have an association. This is one of the first places you should go to seek out help with your job search. Association web sites offer a ton of information related to the industry, and each association has meetings on a regular basis. Attending meetings so you can interact with people in the field is a great way to get started. These individuals will be your most valued supporters and, therefore, the most willing to help you. If you are unable to find a local association specific to your career interests, look into your local business associations, such as the Chamber of Commerce. Many of these organizations offer individuals the chance to attend their meetings and observe. This is a particular good use of your time if any of the member companies employ people in the career you desire. As with all of the other methods above, being prepared when attending association events is a must. Resumés, appropriate attire and being well-versed in your career goals are essential.

Your Career Story: The Key To Your Future

Whether you try one or all of the job hunting methods listed above, the key to your success will lie in the use of your Career Story. Be ready, willing and able to share your story with enthusiasm and clarity. Your ability to articulate your story will have the single biggest impact on your ability to find a job in your chosen career. Why? Sincerity can not be faked. If you are truly interested in finding work in this field, your Career Story will positively reflect it. This quality is so powerful that it draws potential employers to you like a moth to a flame. A person with a clear vision and passion for finding their desired career is an attractive candidate for hire. In summary, take the time to perfect your Career Story before you begin your job hunt. Write it down, read it out loud and try it out on friends and family.

The stronger it is, the better the response from those who hear it. You've come this far in your journey to find career satisfaction; don't waste this opportunity to show others how hard you have worked.

What's Holding You Back?

Ability is what you're capable of doing. Motivation determines what you do. Attitude determines how well you do it.—Lee Holz

Let's recap what you've achieved so far:

1. You've assessed your personal preferences to create a detailed Personal Success Profile.
2. You've used your PSP Summary Sheet to identify and prioritize a group of careers that best suits your unique profile. Furthermore, you have narrowed down the choices, using a customized list of criteria, to help you finally select the right career for you.
3. You've re-invented yourself by creating a resumé that conveys your true skills and abilities in a format that will get you noticed.
4. You've developed a compelling Career Story to help you let everyone you come in contact with understand how and why a career in your chosen field is right for you.

So what's holding you back? Why are you hesitating to start your job hunt? Why aren't you working full force on making your career dream a reality? Perhaps some of the following thoughts are running through your head:

*   I don't have the time right now to look for this job.
*   I'm not really sure I'm ready to make a change at this time.
*   I wish there was an easier way to find a job.
*   I'm just too tired at the end of my work day to look for a different job.

If so, then it's time to recognize that you are making excuses for your fear. Your *NST* is getting the best of you!

NST & Goal Achievement

Change your thoughts, and you change your world.—Norman Vincent Peale

To reach your goal, you must be prepared to step up and make things happen for yourself. No more excuses! Easier said than done, right? Wrong! One of the biggest mistakes people make is the use of negative thoughts that come out in the form of excuses. Most, if not all excuses are not valid. They are based on inaccurate information and false assumptions. The statement, "if there's a will, there's a way" is very true. Excuses are nothing more than self-imposed roadblocks to success. I refer to this in my coaching practice as Negative Self Talk, or NST.

Do you remember the children's story of the little engine that could? The engine was able to climb the hill because it repeated the phrase, "I think I can, I think I can" over and over again. This story is a great example of how to use self-talk effectively. The way the engine spoke to itself provided the motivation needed to achieve its goal. Changing thoughts is the single most significant step people can take to help them achieve their goals. It empowers them to re-define who they are in their minds, a crucial element of success. Ironically, many adults are often surprised to learn that self talk has already played a crucial role in creating who they are today. How? It starts when we are very young. With each experience in life, we unconsciously evaluate it and determine how it impacts us personally. We look at the role we played in the experience and begin to develop an attitude or perception of ourselves for future reference. Let me give you a personal example:

When I was younger, I tried a few sports, but I didn't do very well. My parents didn't do a lot of physical activities or sports either, so over time, through my experiences and surroundings, I came to believe that I wasn't an "athletic" person. In high school, I was a cheerleader, and aside from the occasional aerobics class, I didn't do much else. As I got older and began to feel the need to watch my weight, I always chose to focus on diet because I didn't feel I would ever enjoy exercise. Why? I had convinced myself that I wasn't "athletic" and, therefore, believed I could never be good at exercise.

While studying to become a coach I read some interesting theories about self talk, or, more specifically NST, and realized that I had programmed myself to believe I wasn't "athletic." I immediately decided to see if I was capable of changing my NST. I began by seeking out exercise options I actually considered enjoyable. I joined a gym and attended some group fitness classes that I found to be a lot of fun. Over a period of time, I became the fittest I had been in my whole life. Yet I still didn't feel I could consider myself "athletic." I asked myself what I specifically thought I needed to achieve to dispel this view of myself. I decided that if I was in a position to teach others exercise, then I would have to admit to myself that I was in fact "athletic." So I took a big step and signed up for a course to become a fitness instructor. It was a bit frightening, and at times, I could clearly hear the NST in my head trying to get me to give up. All sorts of excuses would pass through my brain, but I continued on and am now a fitness instructor. I am proud to say that I now consider myself an "athletic" person.

What can be learned from my story? The best way to change NST is to identify the negative statements that are limiting your potential and then attack them head on. Do what it takes to prove that you are capable. Remove the roadblocks to success by identifying what you must do for these negative statements about yourself to no longer be true. In other words, "OWN YOUR ACTIONS!"

When you make excuses for why you can't go after the career path you've worked so hard to identify, you are really just saying that you are afraid to make the effort to succeed. Underneath your excuses lies the truth: You don't think you're capable of making a successful career change. So why put the effort in to making the change occur, right? Stop lying to yourself and recognize that your NST is now the only thing holding you back. Let's take a look specifically at your NST with regards to your career and see what we can do to change it.

NST Exercise

Clear your mind of can't.—Samuel Johnson

The following is an exercise designed to help you identify any negative self talk you are using to hold back from pursuing your career path. Follow these steps to identify what you can do to eliminate your NST.

STEP 1: Check All That Apply

Review the statements below and check off any that you can relate to with respect to your own career situation:

- ❑ I am not ready to make a change in my career.
- ❑ It's too much work to change careers when you are already employed full-time.
- ❑ I don't have time to set up Informational Interviews or do any of the other job hunting methods suggested.
- ❑ I am not good at talking with people.

❑   I feel silly asking people to help me with my career.

❑   I don't feel like I deserve to achieve my career goal.

❑   I'm not talented enough to go into my desired career.

❑   I'm not smart enough to go into my desired career.

❑   I'm not creative enough to go into my desired career.

❑   I'm not strong enough to go into my desired career.

❑   I'm afraid of what people with say if I change careers.

❑   I'm afraid of what people will think if I change careers.

❑   I'm afraid of disappointing my family and friends if I change careers.

❑   I'm afraid of working hard and still not being able to successfully change careers.

❑   I'm afraid I won't be respected if I change careers.

❑   I'm afraid I won't be admired if I change careers.

❑   I'm afraid of changing careers and still not being happy.

Step 2: Add to the List

Now, take a moment to think about your situation and list any additional negative self talk you've been telling yourself with respect to your career. List them in your notebook.

Step 3: Reprogram Your Thoughts

Next, create a table with headings similar to the following one in your notebook. List each of the statements you checked off above as well as any additional statements you listed in your notebook in the first column. Then follow the steps in the subsequent columns to transform these statements into actions and affirmations you can use to support your career efforts. An example has been provided as a guide.

NST Statements	What evidence do you have to support this statement?	What experiences in your past shaped your belief of this statement?	What assumption are you making about your situation?	How could it be a false assumption?	What action can you take to prove to yourself that this statement is false?	How could this statement be rewritten to encourage you?
I am not good at talking about myself with people.	*I'm shy and have a hard time talking to strangers.*	*Growing up, I always hated being in situations where I was forced to introduce myself to people I did not know.*	*People always seemed uninterested or annoyed with me. My family referred to me as the "quiet one" which made me even more self conscious. I don't know how to be "impressive" or "charming."*	*I'm assuming that to be good at talking about myself with others, I need to be really outgoing and charismatic. It's possible to be good at talking to others without being a smooth-talker. There are people who prefer a calm communicator.*	*I can use the Informational Interview process as a way to practice talking to people in order to get more comfortable with discussing myself.*	*Going after my career goal will help me overcome my reluctance to talk about myself with others and help to develop confidence in my own communication style.*

You've just proved to yourself that you can make your chosen career path a reality. Are you still feeling hesitant? It's understandable. You've just completed an exercise that has taken away the security and safety of your excuses. You can't hide behind your NST anymore. The truth is out and you've got no place to go but forward.

Your Past Is Not Your Future

Don't let the fear of striking out hold you back.—Babe Ruth

Isn't it interesting how NST controls us? Just look at all the negative thoughts you had holding you back with respect to your career. Imagine what negative thoughts might be holding you back from some of your other important life goals.

The most valuable lesson I would like you to learn from this section on NST is that your past does not have to be your future. While you may have interpreted past events in your life in such a way that they've subsequently limited what you believe yourself capable of achieving, this does not have to be the case going forward. Assumptions based on past experiences need to be challenged regularly. Why? People change. You aren't the same person you were yesterday. We grow older and wiser with each passing day, and therefore we must recognize that we are more capable with each passing day as well.

Anytime you feel self-doubt or reluctance toward a goal, it's time to assess your NST. Whenever you find yourself making excuses as to why you can't reach a goal, it's time to put your NST on paper. I can't stress it enough: At this point, NST is the only thing holding you back from reaching your dreams. Once you remove it, there is no stopping you.

Taking control of your NST and reprogramming your thoughts is one of the most important ways in which you can take responsibility for your future. "Owning Your Actions" means being ready and willing to put forth the effort required to make change happen. If you are not willing to roll up your sleeves and do the work nec-essary, than you don't deserve to reach your career goal. Want a sure-fire way to hold yourself accountable and get you working on your career goal? Find a Career Mentor.

One Last Tool To Ensure Success: A Career Mentor

If you've taken the time and followed each step in this book, you are almost ready to go forward and make your career goal a reality. However, there is one more resource that you should secure: A Career Mentor. A Career Mentor is someone you can sit down with and share your career goal. You will need to go over all your materials with this person, so get your notebook and papers in order. Why? You are going to want to show them all the things you've learned about yourself through this self-discovery process, as well as all the steps you've taken to determine your goal. You will also want to show them your "New and Improved" resumé and Career Story. Therefore, it is imperative you have everything well-organized before you set up a time to sit down with your Career Mentor.

You might be wondering why I've waited until this point for you to align yourself with a Career Mentor. I have people wait to work with Career Mentors for several reasons. First, you are asking individuals to take time out of their busy schedules to help you. Therefore, you want to make the time they spend with you as productive as possible. Being clear in your self knowledge and prepared to clearly articulate your career goals and how you arrived at them is the best way to show respect to a Career Mentor. Second, showing the amount of time and energy you've put into defining your career goals makes an excellent impression. Career Mentors are more likely to go the extra mile and help you achieve your career goals when they see how much you've already done on your own.

How Do I Choose A Career Mentor?

When identifying and selecting Career Mentors, you want to make sure they can offer the kind of support and resources you need. For example, you do not want to ask individuals to be your Career Mentor if you don't like or respect what they've done with their own career. The point is to work with people who you feel have achieved the kind of career success you are interested in achieving. This does not necessarily mean they must be in the same line of work as your desired career, but that helps. The most important thing is to find a Career Mentor who can provide the kind of support that works best for you. How can you do that? I suggest you review your PSP Summary Sheet to identify which traits would be most beneficial in a Career Mentor. For example, ask yourself the following questions:

*   What kind of Interaction Style would be most helpful to me? Do I want my Career Mentor to have the same Interaction Style as me, or might I need someone with a different style than my own?
*   What are the attributes of career success that I should look for in my Career Mentor?
*   What are the specific elements of guidance and support that I want from my Career Mentor?

Once you've identified what you want in a Career Mentor, it's time to make some phone calls!

How Do I Ask Someone To Be My Career Mentor?

Asking someone to be your Career Mentor is simple. Just use your Career Story as your guide. Share with this person why you are contacting them. Let them know why you are looking for a Career Mentor at this stage in your career search. Most importantly, be specific about the areas of guidance and support you seek. If the individuals you contact don't feel they have the time or ability to mentor you, don't be disappointed. Thank them anyway for taking the time to speak with you and then contact the next person on your list. You should identify at least two or three possible mentors. That way, you're sure to find individuals who are currently able to take time out of their schedules to help you. Don't give up. A Career Mentor is going to play a key role in the next phase of the process: Keeping you motivated and working daily toward your goal.

It's Time To Work

I am always doing things I can't do; that's how I get to do them.—Pablo Picasso

I've given you a lot to consider in this chapter. "Own Your Actions" means stepping up to the plate and doing the work needed to make your career goal come true. I wish success could just fall in to your lap, but aside from a lucky few, the majority of us need to actually work for what we want. Don't worry. The work doesn't have to be overwhelming. With a little strategic planning, you can be on your way to career success in an organized and timely fashion. Let's look at how you can develop a plan to "Work It Daily" in order to reach your goal.

PART IV

THE G.L.O.W. METHOD: Work It Daily

STEP #4: Work It Daily

People often say that motivation doesn't last. Well, neither does bathing—that's why we recommend it daily.—Zig Ziglar

"Work It Daily" simply means you need to re-commit yourself to your goal each and every day. How do you do that? By finding ways to keep your goal in the forefront of your mind so that you'll take steps every day, no matter how small, to get yourself closer to it. Goals are so simple to let slide. Without consistent efforts to achieve them, people find it easy to slack off or make excuses that enable them to give up on their goal. Don't let giving up be your reason for failure. Find a way to work daily on your goal so you can see results that will inspire you to keep going. To do that, you'll need to get organized. So get out that notebook.

Creating a G.L.O.W. Chart

In the business world, when teams work together to define a consistent work process, they often create something called a "flow chart." Since we are going to develop a consistent process that will help you achieve your career goal, I refer to the sheet you are about to create as your "G.L.O.W. Chart." A G.L.O.W. Chart outlines the things you should review and do on a daily basis in order to ensure you stay on track with your goal. Take a look at this G.L.O.W. Chart format and create your own version in your notebook:

GAIN PERSPECTIVE - *Review your PSP Summary Sheet and list all of the personal strengths you believe are going to help you achieve your goal.*

Personal Strengths:
•
•
•

LUMINATE YOUR GOAL – *Write down your final career goal and support its validity by listing how it meets the A.M.P. guidelines.*

Career Goal:

It is Attainable because:
It is Measurable because:
It is Positive because:

OWN YOUR ACTIONS – *List all of the positive career statements you were able to transform from your NST.*

Positive Career Statements
•
•
•
•

WORK IT DAILY – *Create a detailed list of steps you are going to complete in order to achieve your career goal. Identify any resources you will need to help you complete each step. Also list a target date for completing each step. Once completed, you should check off each step in the space provided and move on to the next step. If you find yourself stalling or having trouble completing a particular step, discuss your situation with your Career Mentor to see if they can provide some suggestions to help you.*

ACTION STEPS	Resources Needed	Planned Date for Completion	Completed
1.			
2.			
3.			
4.			
5.			
6.			
7.			
8.			

Your G.L.O.W. Chart provides an at-a-glance look at all of the work you have done with respect to developing your career goal. Reviewing this document regularly will help keep your career goal at the forefront of your mind, enabling you to stay focused on the tasks you need to complete in order to achieve your goal. Each day, you should review this document, adding any additional tasks you've identified as a result of your efforts. By writing these tasks down in the format provided, you will find it easier to motivate yourself to complete them. Don't forget to check them off when each one is completed. There is nothing more gratifying than recognizing an accomplishment, no matter how small, with a big checkmark in the space provided!

Your Personal Motivator

The other reason you should have a Career Mentor at this stage in the process is for the "accountability factor." You've asked this person to provide you with valuable support and guidance, so what should they get in return? That's simple: The chance to see you succeed. You can't let your Career Mentor down. After all the free time and advice they've been willing to give you, you owe it to them to make your career goals happen. Think of it as the added push you need to "Work It Daily." Remember the saying: "You get out what you put in." Make an effort each and every day to move yourself closer to your goal. On those days when you are feeling defeated and unmotivated, reach out to your Career Mentor for support. Talking with a trusted advisor will help you get back on track and focused on your goal. Don't stop now; you've come too far. Don't let all of the hard work of self-discovery and personal planning go to waste. You're in the home stretch!

Patience: The Ultimate Professional Skill

There are no shortcuts to any place worth going.—Beverly Sills

The hardest part from this point forward is the waiting. While you can work each day toward your goal, the reality is that your career goal is not going to happen overnight. Setting up and attending Informational Interviews take time. Networking takes time. Job interviews take time. In other words, the skill you'll need most in this phase of the process is patience. Unfortunately, in a culture that prides itself on instant gratification, the ability to be patient is fast becoming a dying art. When our society's favorite words are, "better, cheaper, faster," how can you possibly be expected to graciously accept the time it takes to move into a new career? You're not alone. Please know that it's completely normal to feel frustrated and anxious with respect to this part of the process. To help combat these feelings I suggest the following two things:

1. As I've stressed earlier, make sure you do something each day to support your career goal. No matter how small the effort, keep yourself on track by working towards your goal on a daily basis.

2. Study the other aspects of your life. Now is the time to focus and enhance some of the other key areas that could use your attention. You've been putting all of your mental energies into developing your career. Take this opportunity to assess how you might be able to improve one of the other areas instead. For example, how's your fitness routine? Could you be working out more? What about your relationship with friends and family? Could you schedule more time with them? What about your physical surroundings? Are your closets or desk due for a good spring cleaning? What about your hobbies? When's the last time you went out and planned something fun? Use this time wisely. Your career goals are going to happen as long as you stay on track. So why not focus some of the energy we've freed up towards something else? You've just completed The G.L.O.W. Method using your career as the focus. Why not use these same resources to develop a game plan for another area of your life? You'll be amazed at how much easier it is to set goals when you've got the right information and tools at your disposal.

Take out that PSP Summary Sheet and use the information you've gathered about yourself to help you create a customized approach to another personal goal you've always wanted but have never been able to attain. You can do it!

Don't Let Others Get You Down

Keep away from small people who try to belittle your ambitions. Small people always do that, but the really great make you feel that you, too, can become great.—Mark Twain

By now you should be feeling real excitement towards the prospect of finding the career satisfaction you want and deserve. You've worked hard to get here and should be very proud of your accomplishments. Unfortunately, not everyone will see your determination to pursue your chosen career path as a good thing. It's sad, but occasionally a client's closest friends and family turn out to be real doomsayers when they tell them what they've learned about themselves and what the client intends to do with respect to their careers. Prepare yourself for the fact that not everyone is going to be enthusiastic about your choices. When you encounter someone who is negative toward your career goals, ask yourself a couple of questions:

- Whose life is it, mine or theirs?
- Does this person have the kind of career success I desire? Are they trying to impose their views on me?
- Is it possible that this person is feeling threatened by my choices? Are they incorrectly viewing my unique career goals as a negative reflection on their own choices?

Remind yourself that you are on the right career track for you. While others may not see it now, they will see it in the future. In the meantime, avoid discussing your career goals with these individuals in order to keep yourself motivated and your relationship with them peaceful. The time will come when your career will no longer be a source of disagreement. You may even be able to show them how to find greater career satisfaction some day.

It's Official – You're G.L.O.W.ing!

If you can dream it, you can do it.—Walt Disney

This is the point where I send you out on your own to make greater career satisfaction a reality. You are ready; I promise. Please know both my company, **J.T. O'Donnell – Career Insights,** and I am here for you. Visit our web site at www.jtodonnell.com to access more information and resources. We'd also love to answer your questions, get your feedback and hear about your success stories. Send an e-mail to info@jtodonnell.com and let us know how you are doing!

Finding a career path that is personally fulfilling does take some work, but as you've just learned, there is a logical and effective way to achieve career satisfaction. I have one last quote to share with you:

In the case of good books, the point is not to see how many of them you can get through, but how many can get through to you.—Mortimer J. Adler

I hope the information in this book inspires you to find the career satisfaction you want and deserve. I encourage you, and anyone you know, not to spend the rest of your life in a "tolerable" career. A satisfying career that supports a successful life is out there for the taking – but only if you reach for it.

J.T.

Printed in the United States
131249LV00014B/212/P